Telekolleg I

Hannelore Gottschalk

Englisch

Units 27–39

Mitarbeit:
Joe Hambrook
Graham Pascoe

Fachliche Beratung:
Hanns Höfer

TR-Verlagsunion

Dieser Band enthält das Arbeitsmaterial zu den 1983 vom Bayerischen Rundfunk produzierten Lehrsendungen »Englisch für Anfänger – Englisch im Telekolleg I«, *Units* 27-39.

Zu diesem Buch gibt es eine Audio-Mitlese-Cassette zur Verbesserung der Aussprache, des Hörverständnisses und der Sprechfertigkeit und eine Audio-Übungs-Cassette mit Übungen aus dem Lehrbuch und Pausen zum Nachsprechen (Komplettpaket Best.-Nr. 24408). Die auf Cassette wiedergegebenen Dialoge beziehungsweise Übungen sind im Buch jeweils durch das Symbol QO gekennzeichnet. Die landeskundlichen Teile in den Units werden durch das Symbol (CB) (cultural background) gekennzeichnet.
Außerdem ist der gesamte Kurs in Originalfassung auch auf Videocassetten lieferbar. Die Audio- und Videocassetten können Sie über Ihre Buchhandlung oder bei der TR-Verlagsunion, Postfach, 80059 München, beziehen.

7. unveränderte Auflage 1994

Fotos: Raimund M. Maxsein, München
Umschlaggestaltung: Beate C. Eberle, München
Zeichnungen: Reiner Stolte und Konrad Wacker, beide München
Gesamtherstellung: Druckerei Gebr. Bremberger, München
ISBN 3-8058-1455-0

VORWORT

Dieses Buch setzt mit den Units 27–39 den Englischkurs im Telekolleg I fort. Das Kernstück jeder Unit ist auch hier wieder die Geschichte. Wie Sie seit der ersten Sendung wissen, verkörpern unsere Schauspieler in jeder Unit neue Personengruppen. Sie spielen also nie „sich selber“. Dadurch werden Sie als Lernende mit Menschen aus den verschiedensten Lebensbereichen zusammengeführt. Das Englisch, das die Schauspieler sprechen, ist jedoch immer ein nachahmenswertes "standard English", wenngleich mitunter örtliche oder soziale Akzente hörbar werden.
In diesem dritten Teil des Lehrgangs kommt auch die so wichtige amerikanische Seite des Englischen zu ihrem Recht. Die Verschiedenartigkeit der durch die Schauspieler verkörperten Charaktere kommt dabei weniger in der Sprache als in der Verhaltensweise (Gestik, Mimik, Grad der Höflichkeit) zum Ausdruck. In den Units 37, 38 und 39, die sich mit dem Thema Amerika befassen, finden Sie die Schreibweise einzelner Wörter in amerikanischem Englisch (American English, AE).
Regisseur und Schauspieler – alle aus Großbritannien und Amerika – wollen Ihnen natürlich eine authentische Sprache und eine authentische Atmosphäre vorführen. Das gilt auch für den Moderator, der Ihnen weiterhin auch deutsche Erklärungen gibt, um den Prozeß des Verstehens abzukürzen. Daß es nicht selten zu humorvollen, ja grotesken Szenen kommt, werden Sie unserem britischen Team nicht übelnehmen. Sie erleben mit, wie sich der sprichwörtliche und mitunter ganz spezielle angelsächsische Humor äußert. Der Lernerfolg, das ist die älteste pädagogische Erfahrung, stellt sich immer dann am nachhaltigsten ein, wenn *instruction* und *entertainment* Hand in Hand gehen. Wir hoffen sogar, daß Sie mit einer gewissen heiteren Erwartung der jeweils nächsten Sendung entgegensehen und Ihnen der Rückblick auf frühere Sendungen manches Schmunzeln entlockt.
Wieder finden Sie den gesamten Dialog im Buch abgedruckt; es kann Ihnen also kein Wort entgehen. In den Dialogen steckt eine Fülle von sorgfältig für Sie ausgewählten Aussagen und Wendungen, die Sie selber beim aktiven Sprechen mit Gewinn verwenden werden. Suchen Sie bitte nach solchen Transferstellen in den Dialogen, die man, losgelöst von der betreffenden Situation, häufig als fertigen Satz gebrauchen kann. (Beispiele: *I'd like to say how grateful I am . . . May I first of all introduce myself . . . It's nearly time to leave . . . There are still some things I want to check etc.)*
Dies ist die Umgangssprache in den englischsprechenden Ländern, keineswegs schulmäßig zurechtgemacht. Damit Sie aber die Sprache als Ganzes assimilieren, nicht nur in einer Auslese von Sprechakten, bieten wir Ihnen in den Sendungen und im Begleitbuch Erklärungen mit Übungen, die auch die Schriftsprache umfassen. Zweck des Buches ist, Ihnen noch deutlicher die sprachlichen Zusammenhänge aufzuzeigen und Sie zum Lösen schriftlicher Fragen und Aufgaben zu ermutigen, wie dies tagtäglich in der Schule geschieht. Bitte vernachlässigen Sie nicht das exakte Wörterlernen, am besten im Satzzusammenhang. Mit jedem neuen Wort, das Sie beherrschen, erhöhen Sie Ihre Fähigkeit zum Verstehen der gesprochenen Sprache und von gedruckten authentischen Texten *(listening comprehension, reading comprehension)*. Beides soll Ihr Ziel sein, dem Sie mit diesem dritten Teil unseres Fernseh-Lehrgangs, dessen sind wir sicher, ein beträchtliches Stück näher kommen werden. Wir wünschen Ihnen weiterhin viel Freude und Erfolg.

Hannelore Gottschalk
Hanns Höfer

INHALTSVERZEICHNIS

Unit	Situation	strukturelle Lernziele	kommunikative Lernziele	Seite
27	**Finding somewhere to live**	– Bruchzahlen – Wiederholungszahlen – Maßangaben – semantische Unterschiede zum Amerikanischen	– eine Wohnung beschreiben (Lage, Größe, Ausstattung) – eine Wohnung mieten oder vermieten – Höhe der Miete nennen – über einen Preis verhandeln – ein Mißverständnis ausräumen – sich für einen Irrtum entschuldigen	7
28	**The professor's speech**	– Self-Pronomen rückbezüglich hervorhebend nach Präpositionen – Gegenseitigkeit: *each other/ one another*	– sich vorstellen – eine berufliche Funktion beschreiben – eine Rede einleiten – Interesse an einer Sache zeigen – sich und andere an etwas erinnern – jdm. etwas anbieten	17
29	**The inventor**	– Bedingungssätze (I) if-Satz Typ 1 und 2 *unless*	– jdm. einen Rat geben – versuchen, jdn. von einer Sache zu überzeugen – eine Bedingung ausdrücken, unter der man etwas gemacht hätte, unter der etwas geschehen wäre – Vorteile einer Sache hervorheben – etwas begründen	27
30	**The editor's office**	– Future Continuous – Future Perfect *till/until* *by* + Terminangabe	– jdm. einen Termin nennen – Vorhaben und Pläne beschreiben – Absichten äußern – widersprechen	36
31	**The election campaign**	– Bedingungssätze (II) if-Satz Typ 3	– jdm. etwas in Aussicht stellen – mögliche Folgen bedenken – sagen, daß man einer Meinung ist – nicht übereinstimmen – hypothetische Bedingungen ausdrücken	45

Unit	Situation	strukturelle Lernziele	kommunikative Lernziele	Seite
32	**The helpful neighbour**	– Hilfsverben (III) und Ersatzformen *must / have to* *can / to be able to* *may / to be allowed to* *ought to / should* *used to*	– Angaben über frühere Tätigkeiten machen – jdn. um Rat fragen – jdn. um einen Gefallen bitten – eine Meinung erfragen – jdm. recht geben – Hilfe anbieten – jdm. einen Fehler oder Irrtum nachsehen	53
33	**At the police station**	– Phrasal verbs *put up with, get rid of, get on with* – Fragepronomen *who, whose, what, which (of)* – verstärkendes *do*	– Empörung ausdrücken – einen Tathergang schildern – um eine Präzisierung bitten – sich höflich entschuldigen – Skepsis äußern	62
34	**Mail order shopping**	– Relativpronomen (I) *who, which, that* – Präpositionen in Relativsätzen	– eine Begründung vorlegen – etwas beschreiben – Interesse bekunden – Preise vergleichen – Kleidergrößen vergleichen – sich schriftlich beschweren – einen Irrtum einsehen	71
35	**A tour of Ireland**	– Relativpronomen (II) *whose* – notwendige Relativsätze – entbehrliche Relativ-sätze – abhängige Fragesätze	– jdn. begrüßen – sich für Landessitten interessieren – um eine Erklärung bitten – einen Rat geben – Wiedersehensfreude ausdrücken – Gastfreundschaft anbieten – jdm. einen Vorschlag machen	79
36	**To buy or not to buy**	– unbestimmte Pronomen *much, many, a lot of, lots of, plenty of, little, few, all, none, each, every, either, any* – Verben mit zwei Objekten – *for* + Objekt + Infinitiv	– jdn. überzeugen – Zweifel oder Ungewißheit ausdrücken – auf Vorzüge hinweisen – jdn. umstimmen – um einen Gefallen bitten – eine Belehrung akzeptieren	90

Unit	Situation	strukturelle Lernziele	kommunikative Lernziele	Seite
37	**In the museum**	– Passiv (I) mit und ohne *by*	– eine Meinung vertreten – Gefallen, Mißfallen ausdrücken – Erstaunen, Überraschung zeigen – jdm. beipflichten – eine gegenteilige Meinung begründen – widersprechen	101
38	**What a way to run an airline**	– Konjunktionen – Kausalsätze – Konzessivsätze – Temporalsätze	– einen Zweck, eine Absicht angeben – einen Vorgang zeitlich und räumlich einordnen – eine Einschränkung machen – eine Reservierung telefonisch bestätigen	110
39	**Out to brunch**	– *would rather / had better* – Besitzfall – s-Genitiv in Verbindung mit Städtenamen und Zeitangaben	– Lebensgewohnheiten vergleichen (GB/USA) – sich im Restaurant sprachlich zurechtfinden – sich nach dem Befinden erkundigen – Komplimente aussprechen und darauf reagieren – etwas vorziehen	120
Alphabetisches Wortschatzregister				129
Aussprachehilfen zu Eigennamen				137
Aussprachehilfen zu Orts- und Ländernamen				138
Erklärung der grammatischen Bezeichnungen				139
Schlüssel zu den Übungen				140

UNIT 27

(CB) Generally people in Great Britain prefer living in their own houses, even if they are quite small. House prices, however, have gone up in the past few years so that it is getting more and more difficult for young people to buy a house of their own. Instead they often rent a flat in one of the many high-rise buildings or tower blocks. They become tenants and every month they pay rent to the owner of the building.

27 A Finding somewhere to live

(J = Jane, R = Russell, a famous pop-star, A = American)

A I'm awfully sorry we're late.
I've only been to this part of London once before.
May we come in?

R That's all right.
We've had a lot of people already.

J But it's still available, I suppose?

R Oh yes. Come in here please.

A Ah, this is the living-room.
What a lovely room!
At least one third larger than the apartment in the Barbican.

J I hope we'll be lucky this time.
After all, we've been unlucky twice so far.

R Would you like to try it?

A Not bad . . .
but it needs tuning.

R Yes, I know.

A Jane, would you measure the windows, please?

J Let me see. They're 5 foot 6 high and 4 foot 9 wide.

A Are those your drapes?
R Drapes, what drapes?
J He means the curtains.
R Oh, the curtains! Yes, of course they're mine!
They cost £29 a yard.
They're new.
A Thank goodness they're yours!
Not my taste at all!
J You'll need a lot of material for these windows about 10 yards.
A That doesn't matter.
My firm will pay at least two thirds of the cost.
R But it will go out through the door, you know . . .
Are you interested in it?
A Yes, I am, very interested.
I like it a lot.
Where does that door lead to?
R That's the kitchen . . .
J A very pleasant kitchen.
A Much pleasanter than the last one.

J We've only seen half of the flat.
Where does the second door lead to?
Ah, the bathroom.
R Yes, that's the bathroom.
Do you want to . . .?
J And the third door . . .
A . . . is the bedroom.
R Yes, that's our bedroom.
A Charming . . . most attractive . . .
Ah, I see you've got central heating as well.
R Yes, of course. It's better for the piano.
The new one is coming soon.
A How much rent do you pay at the moment?
R Rent – for the piano?
J No, what's the rent for this flat?
R Oh, . . . £30.
A That's cheap.
J He means £30 a week. Don't you?
R Of course . . . but the piano . . .
A Is the heating included?
R No, of course not. Heating bills come every quarter.
A Every quarter?
J He means every three months.
A Oh, I see. So it's £30 a week plus heating.

R Well, are you going to take it?
A Let me see . . . when do you have to pay the rent?
On the first or the last of the month?
R The rent? On the 15th of course . . . but are you going to take it?
A That's about £120 a month, £1,440 a year, very reasonable.
And how far is it to the subway?
R The subway? – There isn't one near here.
J He means the Underground.
R Oh, the Underground? The nearest station is three minutes' walk away – but you can't take it by Underground!
You'll need a lorry.
A A what?
R A lorry.
A Oh, a truck!
I'm sure there won't be any problems.
But my firm will arrange all that.
It's very conveniently located.
R Well, I'm afraid I have to go out now.
Do you want it or not?
A Of course I want it. I'll move in on September 1.
R September 1? No, I can't wait that long.
If you want it, you'll have to give me a down payment now and collect it by next Friday.
A Collect it? Collect what?
R The piano, of course!
J Piano? We don't want a piano!
A I've got a piano of my own!

R But you said you were going to take it! I've asked you three times already.

A Yes, I'm going to take your apartment.

R Apartment? What apartment?

J Your flat. He likes your flat.

A You're leaving this fall, aren't you?

R Me – fall? Me leaving? What? Am I?

J This autumn. You're leaving this flat on September 1, aren't you?

R Me leaving this flat? I am not leaving this flat!

A But I said I'm going to take it.

R Yes, the piano, not the flat!

J But this flat is free the weekend after next?

A This is 27 Jervyn Street, isn't it?

R Yes, it is.

A Fifth door on the left, first floor.

R This is not the first floor. This is the ground floor.

J First floor? – Ground floor? Oh dear.

A Ground floor – first floor? Oh, I forgot, we're in Britain.

J So this flat isn't free in September?

R No, it isn't! I wanted to sell my piano. I've just bought a new one!

A And we're looking for a flat.

J How stupid of me! I am sorry!

R That's all right. Mistakes can happen. But you go upstairs in the elevator. The apartment upstairs is the same size as mine. But perhaps you'll like their drapes better than mine!

A Please forgive me. I'm so sorry.

R Don't mention it. It doesn't matter. Perhaps we'll meet again next fall!

J Yes, you'll be neighbours in September.

A Goodbye – please forgive us.

R And we both speak the same language.

1 foot 30,48 cm = 12 inches   1 inch = 2,5 cm   one yard = 3 feet = 0,91 m

£ 29 a yard
£ 120 a month
£ 180 a week
40 miles an hour
the weekend of next

27 B Questions on the story

What does Russell want to sell?
Why did the American visit the wrong flat?
Why does Jane measure the windows?
Is Russell the owner of the flat or the tenant? How can you tell?
What is a down payment?

27 C And you?

What sort of accommodation would you prefer to live in – a high-rise building, a detached or a semi-detached house?
Are you the tenant or the owner of your flat?
How much rent do you pay a month?
Which is better in your opinion – living in a house or a flat? Why?

27 D Fractions — Bruchzahlen

one (a) third	*ein Drittel*
three quarters (fourths)	*drei Viertel*
two fifths	*zwei Fünftel*
seven eighths	*sieben Achtel*
a half	*ein Halbes, eine Hälfte*
two halves	*zwei Halbe, zwei Hälften*

Brüche werden wie im Deutschen gebildet: Grundzahl für den Zähler, Ordnungszahl (vgl. Bd. 1, Unit 3 J) für den Nenner, wobei die Ordnungszahl im Plural die Endung -s hat.

Brüche spricht man wie folgt aus: $\frac{1}{x}$ = one over x [eks]

$\frac{2a}{c + b}$ = two a [eɪ] over c [si:] plus [plʌs] b [bi:].

27 E Write these fractions in words:

4/9 – 2/7 – 3/5 – 1/2 – 2/13 – 7/8 – 5/12 – 1/40 – 3/16 – 6/10

27 F Adverbs of number — Wiederholungszahlen

once	*einmal*
twice	*zweimal*
three times	*dreimal*
four times	*viermal*
eleven times	*elfmal*
a dozen times	*ein dutzendmal*
a hundred times	*einhundertmal*

Wenn wir sagen wollen, wie oft etwas geschieht, verwenden wir die Wiederholungszahlen. Die ersten beiden haben eine eigene Form. Bei allen anderen verwenden wir die Grundzahlen + times. Man spricht 3 x 4 = 12 : Three times four equals twelve *oder:* Three fours are twelve.

27 G Measurements — Maßangaben

1 yard	= 3 feet	= 0.91 metres
1 foot	= 12 inches	= 30.48 centimetres
1 inch	=	2.54 centimetres

Bei Höhenmaßen sagt man in der Umgangssprache meist "foot" statt "feet".
Vor Maß-, Gewichts- oder Zeitangaben steht der unbestimmte Artikel: The curtains cost £29 a yard. The rent is £120 a month. He drives at 40 miles an hour.
Natürlich ist das Dezimalsystem im Kommen. Also:
metre (AE: meter), centimetre, millimetre, kilometre;
litre (AE: liter), gram(me), kilogram(me).
Auch in der Schreibweise gibt es Unterschiede zum Deutschen: Anstelle von 2,54 schreibt man 2.54 und man spricht two point five four. Für Null sagt man in diesem Fall "nought": nought point nine one.

The standard Imperial units of length, Greenwich

27 H How big is the living area of this flat in square feet?

kitchen	11′ x 9′4″
dining-room	10′ x 9′8″
living-room	18′ x 13′6″
bedroom 1	11′6″ x 20′6″
bedroom 2	11′6″ x 11′

total living area:

27 I The months of the year ⊙⊙

January	ˈdʒænjʊərɪ	July	dʒʊˈlaɪ
February	ˈfebrʊərɪ	August	ˈɔːgəst
March	mɑːtʃ	September	sepˈtembə
April	ˈeɪprəl	October	ɒkˈtəʊbə
May	meɪ	November	nəʊˈvembə
June	dʒuːn	December	dɪˈsembə

Beachten Sie: in July, aber: on July 4. Man schreibt July 4, spricht aber "July the fourth" oder "the fourth of July".

The seasons ⊙⊙

spring	autumn (AE = fall)
summer	winter

Monate und Wochentage schreibt man groß, die Jahreszeiten schreibt man klein.

27 J Fill in the correct preposition: ⊙⊙

The flat is . . . . the 5th floor.
They live . . . . 27 Jervyn Street.
The advertisement appeared . . . . . August 8.
They'll move the furniture . . . . lorry.
The American is looking . . . . a flat . . . . London.
Russell looked . . . . the American with surprise.
Russell wants to sell the piano . . . . next week.

27 K Odd word out

Welches Adjektiv paßt nicht in die folgende Gruppe?

charming – pleasant – available – attractive – lovely

Bilden Sie fünf passende Sätze mit diesen Adjektiven.

27 L *Write a letter to a friend of yours. Describe your flat or house, tell your friend about the size, the facilities, the rent you pay (or get), the surroundings, how many people live there, how long you've been living there.*

27 M Differences between British and American English

BE	AE	
curtains	drapes	*Vorhänge*
flat	apartment	*Wohnung*
ground floor	first floor	*Erdgeschoß*
lift	elevator	*Aufzug*
Underground	subway	*Untergrundbahn*
autumn	fall	*Herbst*
lorry	truck	*Lastwagen*

Die Unterschiede treten meist nicht zu stark in Erscheinung. Viele Amerikanismen werden auch in Großbritannien verstanden und sogar gebraucht und umgekehrt.

27 N Situation – Say it in English

Sagen Sie, daß Sie vor einer Dreiviertelstunde angekommen sind.
Sagen Sie, daß Sie einmal im Jahr geschäftlich in London zu tun haben.
Sagen Sie, daß Ihre Miete £200 im Monat beträgt.
Sagen Sie, daß die Zentralheizung in diesem Jahr ein Fünftel mehr kosten wird als im vorigen Jahr.
Sie rufen in einem Immobilienbüro an. Verlangen Sie die Nebenstelle 233. (extension)
Sagen Sie, daß Sie wegen der Anzeige im Lokalblatt anrufen.
Fragen Sie, wie weit es zur nächsten U-Bahn ist.
Fragen Sie, ob Sie die Wohnung am Samstagvormittag besichtigen können.
Sagen Sie, daß Ihnen der Freitagabend auch recht wäre.
Bedanken Sie sich sehr höflich für die Auskünfte. (information)

27 O Summary

Jane is helping an American friend of hers to find a flat in London. They come to Russell's flat at 27 Jervyn Street and begin to look around. Russell is surprised that they want to measure the windows and look in the other rooms – he only wants to sell his piano. The American likes the flat – it's a third larger than another one they saw in the Barbican – and he is pleased to hear that it has central heating. There are, however, a few problems during the discussion, because Russell doesn't understand all the American expressions. For instance, when the American asks how far it is to the subway, Jane has to explain that he means the Underground. But Jane and her friend have misunderstood something too: the flat they wanted to see is on the first floor – an American says "first floor" when an Englishman says "ground floor"! So they've come to the wrong flat.

For sale

Vocabulary			Wortschatz
27	generally	ˈdʒenrəlɪ	im allgemeinen
	even if	ˈi:vən ɪf	wenn . . . auch, selbst, wenn
	however	haʊˈevə	jedoch, indessen
	to go up	tə gəʊ ˈʌp	ansteigen (Preis)
	in the past few years	ɪn ðə ˈpɑ:st fju: ˈjɪəz, ˈjɜ:z	in den vergangenen Jahren, in den letzten Jahren
	so that	səʊ ðət	so daß
	young people	ˈjʌŋ pi:pl	junge Leute
	instead	ɪnˈsted	statt dessen, dafür
	flat *(BE)*	flæt	(Miet-)Wohnung
	high-rise building	ˈhaɪˈraɪz ˈbɪldɪŋ	Hochhaus
	building	ˈbɪldɪŋ	Gebäude
	to become	tə bɪˈkʌm	werden
	tenant	ˈtenənt	Mieter, Pächter
	rent	rent	Miete
	owner	ˈəʊnə	Eigentümer, Inhaber
27 A	once	wʌns	einmal
	available	əˈveɪləbl	verfügbar
	at least	ət ˈli:st	zumindest, mindestens
	one third	wʌn ˈθɜ:d	ein Drittel
	apartment *(AE)*	əˈpɑ:tmənt	(Miet-)Wohnung
	so far	səʊ ˈfɑ:	bisher, bis jetzt
	not bad	nɒt ˈbæd	nicht übel, nicht schlecht
	tuning	ˈtju:nɪŋ, *(AE)* tu:nɪŋ	(Ein-)Stimmen
	to measure	tə ˈmeʒə	ausmessen
	foot (pl feet)	fʊt (fi:t)	Fuß (= 12 Zoll = 30,48 cm)
	high	haɪ	hoch
	wide	waɪd	breit
	drapes *(AE)*	dreɪps	Vorhänge
	curtains *(BE)*	ˈkɜ:tnz	Vorhänge
	a yard	ə ˈjɑ:d	ein Yard (= 0,91 m)
	taste	teɪst	Geschmack
	at all	əˈtɔ:l	durchaus, überhaupt
	firm	fɜ:m	Firma
	cost	kɒst	Kosten
	to lead to	tə li:d ˈtʊ	hinführen zu
	pleasant	ˈpleznt	gemütlich, schön
	bathroom	ˈbɑ:θrʊm, ˈbɑ:θru:m	Bad(ezimmer)
	bedroom	ˈbedrʊm, ˈbedru:m	Schlafzimmer
	attractive	əˈtræktɪv	anziehend, hübsch
	central heating	ˈsentrəl ˈhi:tɪŋ	Zentralheizung
	quarter	ˈkwɔ:tə	Vierteljahr
	plus	plʌs	und, plus, zuzüglich

	reasonable	ˈriːznəbl	vernünftig
	subway	ˈsʌbweɪ	*(BE)* Unterführung *(AE)* Untergrundbahn
	walk	wɔːk	Weg
	three minutes' walk	ˈθriː mɪnɪts ˈwɔːk	cin Wcg von drei Minuten
	away	əˈweɪ	weg, entfernt
	lorry *(BE)*	ˈlɒrɪ	Lastwagen
	truck *(AE)*	trʌk	Lastwagen
	I'm sure	aɪm ˈʃʊə, ˈʃɔː	ich bin sicher, überzeugt
	to arrange	tʊ əˈreɪndʒ	regeln, arrangieren, in Ordnung bringen
	convenient	kənˈviːnjənt	angenehm, passend
	conveniently located	kənˈviːnjəntlɪ ləʊˈkeɪtɪd	günstig gelegen
	down payment	ˈdaʊn ˈpeɪmənt	Anzahlung
	to collect	tə kəˈlekt	abholen
	three times	ˈθriː ˈtaɪmz	dreimal
	fall *(AE)*	fɔːl	Herbst
	autumn *(BE)*	ˈɔːtəm	Herbst
	first floor *(AE)*	ˈfɜːst ˈflɔː	Erdgeschoß
	ground floor *(BE)*	ˈgraʊnd ˈflɔː	Erdgeschoß
	mistake	mɪˈsteɪk	Fehler
	upstairs	ʌpˈsteəz	nach oben; das obere Stockwerk
	elevator *(AE)*	ˈelɪveɪtə	Aufzug
	lift *(BE)*	lɪft	Aufzug
	to forgive	tə fəˈgɪv	verzeihen
	neighbour	ˈneɪbə	Nachbar
27 B	to mix up	tə mɪks ˈʌp	verwechseln, durcheinanderbringen
	term	tɜːm	Begriff, Ausdruck
	in advance	ɪn ədˈvɑːns	im voraus
	deposit	dɪˈpɒzɪt	An-, Einzahlung
27 C	accommodation	əkɒməˈdeɪʃn	Unterkunft
27 D	fractions	ˈfrækʃnz	Bruchzahlen
27 F	to equal	tʊ ˈiːkwəl	ergeben, ausmachen *(Mathematik)*
27 G	measurements	ˈmeʒəmənts	Maße, Maßangaben
	inch	ɪntʃ	Zoll (= 2,54 cm)
	metre (*AE* meter)	ˈmiːtə	Meter
	centimetre (*AE* centimeter)	ˈsentɪmiːtə	Zentimeter
	millimetre (*AE* millimeter)	ˈmɪlɪmiːtə	Millimeter
	kilometre (*AE* kilometer)	ˈkɪləmiːtə, kɪˈlɒmɪtə	Kilometer
	litre (*AE* liter)	ˈliːtə	Liter
	gram(me)	græm	Gramm
	nought	nɔːt	Null *(Mathematik)*

27 H	living area	ˈlɪvɪŋ eərɪə	Wohnfläche
	total	ˈtəʊtl	gesamt
	square foot	skweə ˈfʊt	Quadratfuß
27 I	season	ˈsi:zn	Jahreszeit
	spring	sprɪŋ	Frühling, Frühjahr
27 J	to appear	tʊ əˈpɪə	erscheinen
	furniture	ˈfɜ:nɪtʃə	Möbel
27 K	odd	ɒd	unpassend
27 L	facilities	fəˈsɪlətɪz	Einrichtungen, Anlagen
	surroundings	səˈraʊndɪŋz	Umgebung
27 M	difference	ˈdɪfrəns	Unterschied
27 N	extension	ɪkˈstenʃn	Nebenstelle
	advert (= advertisement)	ˈædvɜ:t	Anzeige
	information	ɪnfəˈmeɪʃn	Auskünfte
27 O	pleased	pli:zd	erfreut
	expression	ɪkˈspreʃn	Ausdruck
	for instance	fr ˈɪnstəns	zum Beispiel
	to misunderstand	tə mɪsʌndəˈstænd	mißverstehen

UNIT 28

The Tower of London

CB The Tower of London is one of the most interesting buildings in Britain. It stands just outside the City on the north bank of the Thames.

In its 900-year history, it has been a fortress, a royal palace, a zoo, and above all a state prison.

In 1078 William the Conqueror began to build the Tower to show his power over the city. The oldest part of the fortress is the White Tower. Inside the White Tower is St. John's Chapel – a beautiful example of Norman architecture. The inner and outer walls followed in the 13th century and the Bloody Tower in the 14th century. Among the famous prisoners who have ended their days here were King Henry VI, King Edward V, and the second and fifth wives of King Henry VIII (Anne Boleyn and Catherine Howard). Sir Thomas More, the great humanist and Lord Chancellor of Henry VIII, and Sir Walter Raleigh, the famous explorer, were also imprisoned here before they were beheaded. Nowadays the Tower houses the National Collection of Arms and Armour and of course you can see the Crown Jewels and other regalia used at coronations.

The men who guard the Tower and the valuable Crown Jewels are the Yeomen Warders. They wear traditional Tudor uniforms.

28 A The professor's speech

(J = Jane, R = Russell)

R Ladies and Gentlemen:
I'd like to begin by saying . . .
. . . once again
I'd like to say how grateful I am for

R your invitation to speak to you tonight.
May I first of all introduce myself –
my name's Russell Grant, and I'm
Professor of History at London University.

R My subject tonight, the Tower of London, is, I'm sure you'll agree, one of the most interesting buildings in Britain.
When we step through the outer gates, we find ourselves in the Middle Ages.
Hmm. That sounds silly.
We don't find ourselves in the Middle Ages, we find ourselves in the Tower of London.
I must change that . . .
When we step through the outer gates, we find ourselves in Water Lane . . .
Is that right? I can't remember . . .
Is it Water Lane or Mint Street?
I just can't remember! I must look that up before tonight.

(Enter Jane with pot of tea)

J How are you getting on, dear?
It's nearly time to leave.
Who were you talking to?

R Oh, I was just talking to myself – I was just reciting my speech to myself. There are still some things I want to check – maybe you could help me on one or two, let me see . . .
Ah yes – imagine you're going through the outer gates into the Tower of London . . .

The Traitors' Gate in the Tower

J Yes . . .

R Are you in Water Lane or Mint Street?

J I really don't know, dear. You're the Professor of History, not me.
Are you ready to leave now?

R Yes, I'm more or less ready.
But I can't remember my speech – I think this evening's going to be a disaster.

J Nonsense, dear. I'm sure the members of the Women's Institute and their husbands will all enjoy themselves immensely. It isn't often that they have a real professor to talk to them.
And I'm sure you'll enjoy yourself too.
Help yourself to some tea.

R Hmm. I'm sure it'll be a terribly embarrassing evening. Now, I asked you to remind me of something – what was it?

J You asked me to remind you to take your glasses.

R Ah, that was it – thank you so much.

J You must hurry. It's late.

R Don't worry, Jane.
I'm ready. I've washed, I've shaved.

J And you've hurt yourself.

R Yes, I cut myself with the razor.

J You should be more careful when you're shaving.
Your bow tie!

R Yes, I tied it myself.
Thank you.

J Can you remember your speech?

R Oh dear, I'm sure I'll forget my speech.
I wrote it myself, but I still don't know it!

J You wrote it yourself, but it's a good job you didn't type it yourself – your typing's even worse than your writing.
Here's the typed copy – I typed it while you were washing and shaving.

R Ah, thank you, Jane – you're wonderful.

J Well, you helped me with my speech last week, so I helped you with yours. Life's so much easier when people help each other instead of fighting against each othcr all the time!

R Well, I know I'm going to make a terrible fool of myself tonight.

J Nonsense, your audience will enjoy themselves enormously.

R I feel a bit sick.

J Help yourself to some more tea.

R I really feel quite ill. I think I've caught a cold.

J Well, you played golf for three hours in the rain yesterday.
So you've caught a cold.
When you begin your speech, you must apologise for having a cold.
They'll understand.

R I really feel terrible.

J I'm sure you'll be quite all right.
You must hurry. You've got to dress.
The meeting starts at half past six.

R All right. Where's the jacket?

J I'll fetch it.

R That speech!
I wrote it myself and I said it to myself, but I can't remember it. My head!
I must pull myself together.

J Here's your jacket.

R Thank you.
I don't like this dinner-jacket.
I don't feel comfortable in it.

J Why? You look splendid.

R But I can't move in it. (jacket splits)

J Good heavens! You've torn it.

R Damn!

J You can't give a speech in a jacket like this.

R And with a cold too.

J Well, I'll just have to give the speech for you!

R What do you mean?
You don't know anything about the subject.

J Oh yes I do. I typed out your speech from beginning to end! I know it off by heart! Listen!
Ladies and Gentlemen: First of all I'd like to apologise for my husband, who's caught a cold and can't come tonight – I'll do my best to replace him.
My subject tonight, the Tower of London, is, I'm sure you'll agree, one of the most interesting buildings in Britain . . .

William the Conqueror, The Bayeux Tapestry

28 B Questions

What has the Tower been in its long history?
What can you see in the Tower of London?
Who began to build the Tower?
Name two famous prisoners who died in the Tower.
What's Russell's job in the story?
What had Russell been doing before Jane brought the tea?
Russell hurt himself. How did he do it?
Why does Russell not like his dinner-jacket?
When does the meeting at the Women's Institute start?
Why can't Russell go there?

28 C And you?

Which sights would you like to visit in London?
Which sights would you show a foreign visitor in your home town?

28 D Self-pronouns

Pronomen mit "-self"

I	–	**myself**	we	–	**ourselves**
you	–	**yourself**	you	–	**yourselves**
he	–	**himself**	they	–	**themselves**
she	–	**herself**			
it	–	**itself**			

Dem unbestimmten Pronomen "one" entspricht "oneself".

28 E Use of self-pronouns

a) rückbezüglich

May I introduce **myself?**	*Darf ich mich vorstellen?*
He cut **himself** with his razor.	*Er schnitt sich mit seinem Rasiermesser.*
The children enjoyed **themselves.**	*Die Kinder vergnügten sich.*

Die self-Pronomen sind hier rückbezüglich, weil Subjekt und Objekt ein und dieselbe Person sind: May I (S) introduce myself (O)?

28

b) hervorhebend

I've seen it **myself.**	*Ich habe es selbst gesehen.*
He tied his bow tie **himself.**	*Er hat seine Schleife selbst gebunden.*
She made the cake all by **herself.**	*Sie hat den Kuchen ganz allein gemacht (gebacken).*

Das self-Pronomen dient auch zur Verstärkung oder Hervorhebung eines Substantivs oder Pronomens. Es wird dann verwendet, wenn man sagen will, daß man etwas selbst, allein, ohne fremde Hilfe gemacht hat. Das self-Pronomen kann hier hinter dem Wort stehen, das man besonders hervorheben will, oder am Ende des Satzes.

c) nach Präpositionen

He was talking to **himself.**	*Er sprach zu sich.*
You ought to be ashamed of **yourself.**	*Du solltest dich schämen.*

28 F Rückbezüglich im Deutschen, kein self-Pronomen im Englischen

He turned round.	*Er drehte sich um.*
They sat down.	*Sie setzten sich.*

Zu den bisher bekannten, im Englischen nicht rückbezüglichen Verben gehören:

to apologise	*sich entschuldigen*
to afford	*sich leisten*
to be afraid	*sich fürchten*
to be angry	*sich ärgern*
to be glad	*sich freuen*
to apply for	*sich bewerben um, für*
to change	*sich (ver)ändern*
to catch a cold	*sich erkälten*
to complain about	*sich beschweren über*
to decide	*sich entschließen*
to enquire	*sich erkundigen*
to happen	*sich ereignen*
to hurry	*sich beeilen*
to meet	*sich treffen, sich begegnen*
to move	*sich bewegen*
to worry about	*sich Sorgen machen über, um*

28 G Fill in -self/-selves where necessary: QO

They enjoyed .... at the party.
We found .... in the wrong flat.
I can't remember .... your name.
He's caught .... a cold.
She introduced .... to the audience.
I must apologise .... for being late.
He sat .... down.
Help .... to a cigarette.
You've got to dress ....
He hurt .... with his razor.
Have we got to do it all by .... ?
She cut .... with a knife the other day.
He can't afford .... to buy a new jacket at the moment.

28 H each other / one another

They are talking to **each other.**	*Sie reden gerade miteinander, einer mit dem anderen.*
These men hate **one another.**	*Diese Männer hassen sich gegenseitig, einer den anderen.*

Die Gegenseitigkeit drückt man im Englischen mit "each other" bzw. "one another" aus.

28 I Complete the following sentences with "each other" or a self-pronoun: QO

Russell couldn't control ....
The two men didn't get on very well. In fact, they disliked ....
They shouted at ....
The one sitting opposite Russell couldn't pull .... together.
They saw .... in the mirror.
The members introduced .... to ....

28 J Give the German equivalents of these phrases:

She worried about his health.
They met yesterday.
Don't move.
You've changed a lot.
They love each other very much.
I hope you remember him.
Just fancy! I've won £1,000 on the football pools.
Did you enjoy yourselves at the party?

Always try to be yourself.
This morning I washed and shaved quickly. Then I got dressed.
They shook hands with each other.

28 K Is it "remind" or "remember"?

You asked me to . . . . . . you about the meeting.
Do you . . . . what time it starts?
I must . . . . to take my glasses with me.
It's a good thing you . . . . . . me to take my books.
"We . . . . visitors that the Tower gates close at five o'clock."

28 L Which definition or synonym goes with each word?

to measure	to say you don't like something
to check	to say you're sorry
to complain	to find out the exact size
immense	to imagine something
to apologise	to have the same opinion
splendid	enormous
to agree	to check something is right
	wonderful
	terrible
	to have a different opinion

28 M *Write a short speech yourself – introduce yourself and tell the audience some details about your home town. Describe some interesting people who live there.*

28 N Situation – Say it in English

Bieten Sie jemandem noch etwas Tee an.
Sagen Sie Ihrem Gast, er möge sich mit Kuchen bedienen.
Sagen Sie, daß Sie sich nicht mehr an den Namen Ihres Nachbarn erinnern können.
Bitten Sie jemanden, Sie daran zu erinnern, Ihre Brille mitzunehmen.
Sagen Sie, daß Sie sich in diesem Anzug (Kostüm) nicht wohl fühlen.
Sagen Sie, daß Sie sich erkältet haben, als Sie gestern abend im Regen nach Hause gingen.
Sagen Sie, daß Sie sich bei der morgigen Konferenz nicht blamieren möchten.
Empfehlen Sie Ihrem Gesprächspartner, etwas vorsichtiger zu sein.
Entschuldigen Sie sich, daß Sie zu spät dran sind.
Sie glauben, daß dieser Abend ein Reinfall werden wird.

28 O Summary

Mr Grant is a famous Professor of History at London University. Tonight he has to give a talk at the Women's Institute about the Tower of London. He is reading his speech to himself when his wife comes in with some tea. The professor is worried. Although he wrote the speech himself, he can't remember it. He is afraid he will make a fool of himself at the meeting. His wife tries to make him feel better. The problem is that he has also caught a bad cold and doesn't like his bow tie and dinner-jacket. The disaster is complete when he puts his jacket on and tears it. He can't give the speech after all. Luckily his wife can help him. She is not a Professor of History but she has typed out the speech for her husband, so she knows it off by heart. She tells him not to worry because she can give the speech instead of her husband.

Where's the Tower?

Vocabulary			Wortschatz
28	bank	bæŋk	Ufer
	above all	ə'bʌv 'ɔ:l	vor allem, hauptsächlich
	prison	'prɪzn	Gefängnis
	power	'paʊə	Macht, Stärke, Herrschaft
	chapel	'tʃæpl	Kapelle
	Norman	'nɔ:mən	(Adj) normannisch; (S) Normanne, Normannin
	architecture	'ɑ:kɪtektʃə	Architektur
	inner	'ɪnə	innere; Innen-
	outer	'aʊtə	äußere; Außen-
	to follow	tə 'fɒləʊ	folgen
	prisoner	'prɪznə	Gefangene(r)
	humanist	'hju:mənɪst	Humanist, Menschenkenner
	Lord Chancellor	lɔ:d 'tʃɑ:nsələ	Lordkanzler
	explorer	ɪk'splɔ:rə	Forscher
	to imprison	tʊ ɪm'prɪzn	gefangenhalten, einsperren
	nowadays	'naʊədeɪz	heutzutage
	to house	tə 'haʊz	unterbringen
	collection	kə'lekʃn	Sammlung
	arms	ɑ:mz	Waffen
	armour	'ɑ:mə	(hist.) Rüstung
	regalia	rɪ'geɪljə	Krönungsinsignien, Kronjuwelen
	coronation	kɒrə'neɪʃn	Krönung
	to guard	tə 'gɑ:d	bewachen
	uniform	'ju:nɪfɔ:m	Uniform

28 A	speech	spiːtʃ	Rede
	gentleman, pl gentlemen	ˈdʒentlmən, ˈdʒentlmən	Herr, pl. Herren
	grateful	ˈgreɪtfʊl	dankbar
	to introduce o.s.	tʊ ɪntrəˈdjuːs	sich vorstellen
	subject	ˈsʌbdʒɪkt, ˈsʌbdʒəkt	Thema
	to agree	tʊ əˈgriː	zustimmen, einverstanden sein, einwilligen
	to step through	tə step ˈθruː	hindurchgehen
	gate	geɪt	Tor
	to sound	tə ˈsaʊnd	klingen, sich anhören
	to look s.th. up	tə lʊk ˈʌp	etwas nachschauen
	to get on	tə get ˈɒn	zurechtkommen, weiterkommen
	nearly	ˈnɪəlɪ	fast, beinahe
	to recite	tə rɪˈsaɪt	auf-, hersagen
	to imagine	tʊ ɪˈmædʒɪn	sich vorstellen
	disaster	dɪˈzɑːstə	Katastrophe, Unheil
	member	ˈmembə	Mitglied
	institute	ˈɪnstɪtjuːt	Institut, Einrichtung
	immense	ɪˈmens	ungeheuer, prächtig
	real	rɪəl	echt
	to help o.s. to	tə help ˈtʊ	sich bedienen mit, sich nehmen
	embarrassing	ɪmˈbærəsɪŋ	lästig, hinderlich
	to remind someone of s.th.	tə rɪˈmaɪnd ˈɒv	jdn. an etwas erinnern
	glasses	glɑːsɪz	Brille
	to wash	tə ˈwɒʃ	sich waschen
	to shave	tə ˈʃeɪv	sich rasieren
	to hurt o.s.	tə ˈhɜːt	sich verletzen
	to cut o.s.	tə kʌt	sich schneiden
	razor	ˈreɪzə	Rasiermesser
	bow tie	ˈbəʊ ˈtaɪ	(Frack-)Schleife, Fliege
	to tie	tə ˈtaɪ	binden
	to type	tə ˈtaɪp	mit der Maschine schreiben, tippen
	copy	ˈkɒpɪ	Abschrift, Kopie
	to fight against each other	tə ˈfaɪt	sich gegenseitig bekämpfen
	to make a terrible fool of oneself	tə meɪk ə ˈterəbl ˈfuːl	sich schrecklich blamieren
	fool	fuːl	Narr, Dummkopf
	audience	ˈɔːdjəns	Publikum, Zuhörer(schaft)
	enormous	ɪˈnɔːməs	riesig, enorm, gewaltig
	sick	sɪk	unwohl, kränklich
	rain (S)	reɪn	Regen
	to apologise	tʊ əˈpɒlədʒaɪz	sich entschuldigen

	to dress	tə 'dres	sich anziehen
	to fetch	tə 'fetʃ	holen
	to pull o.s. together	tə pʊl tə'geðə	sich zusammennehmen, -reißen
	dinner-jacket	'dɪnə dʒækɪt	Smoking
	to tear	tə 'teə	zerreißen
	to type out	tə taɪp 'aʊt	mit der Maschine abschreiben, abtippen
	to know s.th. off by heart	tə 'nəʊ ɒf baɪ 'hɑːt	etwas auswendig kennen, wissen
	to replace s.b.	tə rɪ'pleɪs	jdn. ersetzen
28 B	to die	tə 'daɪ	sterben
28 C	sights	saɪts	Sehenswürdigkeiten
28 E	to be ashamed of	tə bɪ ə'ʃeɪmd əv	sich schämen
28 F	to turn round	tə tɜːn 'raʊnd	sich umdrehen
28 I	to control o.s.	tə kən'trəʊl	sich beherrschen, sich in der Gewalt haben
	to shout	tə 'ʃaʊt	schreien
	opposite	'ɒpəzɪt	gegenüber
28 J	Just fancy!	dʒʌst 'fænsɪ	Denken Sie nur! Stell dir vor!
	to shake hands	tə ʃeɪk 'hændz	die Hände schütteln, die Hand geben
28 N	to be at ease	tə biː ət 'iːz	sich wohlfühlen
28 O	complete	kəm'pliːt	vollständig

UNIT 29

29

(CB) Many British people enjoy inventing things as a hobby. There are many great inventions and discoveries which come from Britain. In the 18th century, the age of the Industrial Revolution, James Watt, a Scot, developed the steam-engine and in the early 19th century George Stephenson invented the first locomotive. In 1825 the first railway with Stephenson's locomotive ran from Stockton to Darlington.
The textile industry developed through the invention of the power-loom by Edmund Cartwright. James Hargreaves invented a spinning-machine. Another famous name is Alexander Fleming, also a Scot, who discovered penicillin. Alexander Bell, an American who originally came from Scotland, invented the telephone in 1876.
All sorts of inventions – not only British ones – are displayed in the Science Museum in London. There you can also see the latest developments in electronics, space flight, photography, printing or nuclear physics.

29 A The inventor

(J = Jane, R = Russell)

(R reading letter)

R Dear Mr Grant,
Thank you very much for your letter.
We are very interested in your inventions. If it is convenient for you, our household-gadget expert, Dr J. Egan, will visit you on Wednesday, 19th March at 11 a.m.
Yours sincerely,
Western Gadgets Ltd.

James Watt

R Hm. I wonder when he's coming. He's not very punctual. If he's not here by 11.15, I'll go and do the shopping.
Ah. Perhaps that's him now.
Oh. Good morning.

J Good morning. I'd like to speak to Mr Grant.

R That's me. What can I do for you?

J I've got an appointment to see you. I'm from Western Gadgets Limited.

R Oh, but I was expecting Dr Egan . . .

J That's right. That's me.

R Oh. Pleased to meet you. Do come in. Would you like to sit down?

J Ah, this is one of your inventions, isn't it?
If I needed a new armchair, this would be just the thing. Have you already sold the idea to anybody?

R No, not yet.

J Well, if you showed me how to sit up straight, we could talk business.

R Yes, of course. I'm so sorry.
If you want to lie down, you press this button and if you want to sit up, you press this one.

J Very interesting. A good idea.

R Would you like something to drink?
That's my remote-controlled drink bar over there.

J Remote-controlled?

R Yes, you don't have to get up.
This is the control panel.
You can choose from tea, coffee, orange juice or milk.
If you press this button, it'll make black coffee.

J And if I pressed this button – MILK –, it would make white coffee?

R No, you'd get milk.
But if you want white coffee, press the two buttons COFFEE and MILK.

J All right, I'd like white coffee . . .

J so I'll press COFFEE and MILK together.

R Now you can just sit here and wait. You don't have to do anything else.

J It would be useful if we had a machine like this in our office.
Did you invent this yourself?

R Yes, I invented it a few years ago.

J And have you sold many of them?

R Well, not yet.

J Why not?

R Nobody wanted to buy it.

J Perhaps my firm might be interested in it if . . .

R Oh dear, if there's not enough water in it, it won't make proper coffee . . .
Yes, there was enough water . . .
Here you are, your coffee.

J Hmm. I see. If you connected the machine to the tap, you'd always have enough water and that wouldn't happen.

R Yes, but if I connected the machine to the tap, I couldn't use the tap . . .
but I'll try that. Thanks for the tip.

R Are you an inventor too?

J No, no. I just advise the company on new inventions.
If you improved this machine a little, we might buy it.

R Yes, I'm sure I could improve it . . .

J Is this the only work you do?

R Inventing you mean? Yes, it is.

J How do you earn your living?

R Well, my wife goes out to work.
She works at the local library.
She's a trained librarian you know.

J I see. And you earn money from your inventions?

R Well, not exactly. I haven't sold any yet.
If I sold two inventions a year, I could earn enough money for both of us.

J I see.

J If I were you, I'd try and get a regular job.

R I see what you mean.
If I worked for a firm, I'd earn a monthly salary.

J Yes, you would.

R And if I worked for a firm, I could make much better machines because I'd have better tools and a larger workshop. But nobody wants inventors these days.

J Oh yes they do! We're always looking for good ideas.
What's your latest invention?

R Well, at the moment I'm working on an automatic page-turner, you know, to turn over the pages when you're reading in bed.

J I'm sure that would sell.
If you were interested in a job with us, you could apply to our Research and Development Department.

R You mean I could send an application for a job to your company?

29

J Yes, that's right. Send your application to Mr Jim Faraday.

R Jim Faraday? What does he look like? Is he tall and dark?

J Yes, he is. Why?

R If he used to be a teacher at Leeds Grammar School, he's probably my former physics teacher. And I'm afraid I wasn't very good at physics.

J Don't worry, professors are very forgetful.

R I'm not so sure.

29 B Questions

Who developed the steam-engine?
In what century did he build his steam-engine?
Where in London can you see some famous inventions?
Who invented the power-loom?
Who built the first telephone?
Does Russell make a living from his inventions?
How many inventions has he sold so far?
What does Russell's wife do to earn a living?
What's Russell's latest invention?
What could Russell do to improve his situation?
Who's Jim Faraday?
What do you know about Michael Faraday?

29 C And you?

Are you good at physics?
Are you interested in electronics?
Is photography your hobby?
Can you think of any modern invention?
Which invention, in your opinion, has caused the most problems? Why?

29 D Conditional clauses (I) — Bedingungssätze

Type 1

if-clause: present	main clause: will-future can, must imperative
If you **press** this button, *Wenn Sie auf diesen Knopf drücken,*	it'**ll** make black coffee. *wird sie (= die Maschine) schwarzen Kaffee machen.*
If you **haven't got** enough money, *Wenn Sie nicht genug Geld haben,*	you **can't** buy the car. *können Sie sich das Auto nicht kaufen.*
If you **want** to lie down, *Wenn Sie sich hinlegen wollen,*	**press** this button. *drücken Sie auf diesen Knopf.*

Wenn wir uns die Bedingung ganz konkret vorstellen, verwenden wir Typ 1: im if-Satz die Gegenwart, im Hauptsatz die Zukunft mit "will", die Hilfsverben "can" oder "must" oder den Imperativ.

Type 2

if-clause: simple past	main clause: would could might
If I **pressed** this button, *Wenn ich auf den Knopf drücken würde (drückte),*	it **would make** proper coffee? *würde sie richtigen Kaffee machen?*
If I **were** you, *Wenn ich du wäre,*	**I'd buy** the car. *würde ich das Auto kaufen.*
If I **sold** two inventions a year, *Wenn ich zwei Erfindungen pro Jahr verkaufen würde,*	I **could earn** enough money. *könnte ich genug Geld verdienen.*
If you **improved** this machine a little, *Wenn Sie diese Maschine etwas verbessern würden,*	we **might buy** it. *würden wir sie vielleicht kaufen.*

Wenn wir uns die Bedingung nur theoretisch vorstellen, verwenden wir Typ 2: im if-Satz die einfache Vergangenheit, im Hauptsatz "would", wenn wir die Folgen etwas behutsamer ausdrücken möchten "could" oder "might".
Eine Besonderheit gibt es bei dem Verb "to be": Bei Typ 2 sagen wir nach "if" für alle Personen "were".

29

29 E Complete the sentences with the correct tense: QO

If you hurry, you .... the train. (catch)
We .... you to stay if we had a larger house. (invite)
You'd learn English more quickly if you .... to Britain. (go)
He would enjoy this if he .... here. (be)
If you .... interested in a job, you could send your application to our Research Department. (be)
Would he get angry if I .... him about it? (tell)
Don't miss the Science Museum if you .... to London. (go)
If you don't hurry, you .... late. (be)
If you ...., he will never speak to you again. (not apologise)
If you .... help me, I would be very grateful. (can)

29 F unless

We won't buy your invention **unless** you improve it.

"Unless" steht hier gleichberechtigt für "if not": We won't buy your invention if you don't improve it.

Verwenden Sie "unless" anstelle von "if not": QO

You can't buy the refrigerator if you haven't got the money.
You can't drive a car if you haven't passed your driving test.
You won't pass your examination if you don't work hard.
I'll be in London by 5 o'clock if I don't miss the train.
It won't make proper coffee if there isn't enough water in it.

29 G "if" / "when"

I'm sure he'll leave his job **if** he finds a better one.
Ich bin sicher, er wird seine Stellung aufgeben, wenn er eine bessere findet.
You'll speak English well **when** our course ends.
Sie werden gut Englisch sprechen, wenn unser Kurs zu Ende ist.

"If" verwenden wir für Ereignisse, die uns möglich erscheinen, "when" verwenden wir für Ereignisse, die absolut sicher eintreffen oder für Aussagen, die immer gültig sind.

29 H Ask your friends what they would do if . . .

- live in London
- be President of the USA
- have a million dollars
- get a ticket for speeding
- hear a burglar in your neighbour's flat
- be late for a meeting
- the price of petrol be double what it is now

29 I Write down your friends' answers to your questions (29 H):

Example — Beispiel

> What would you do if you lived in London? –
> If I lived in London, I'd have an English breakfast every morning.

29 J Which definition or synonym goes with the words in list 1?

list 1	list 2
to wonder	helpful
to speak to	real
to expect	to ask oneself
useful	to talk to
proper	the pay for a month's work
to improve	to wait for
salary	to make better
	to be surprised

29 K A practical invention

Write a short report about an invention you'd buy for your household. Give reasons why you'd buy it and state the advantages.

29 L Situation – Say it in English

Sagen Sie, daß Sie Herrn X sprechen möchten.
Sagen Sie, daß Sie eine Verabredung mit ihm haben.
Wie drückt Ihr Gesprächspartner seine Freude darüber aus, Ihnen zu begegnen, Sie zu treffen?
Sagen Sie, daß es nützlich wäre, wenn Sie in Ihrem Büro eine derartige Maschine hätten.

Sagen Sie, daß Ihre Firma eventuell daran interessiert wäre.
Raten Sie Ihrem Gesprächspartner, diese Maschine zu verbessern.
Sagen Sie, daß Sie überzeugt sind, daß sie sich dann verkaufen würde (ließe).
Ihr Gesprächspartner möchte wissen, wie Sie Ihren Lebensunterhalt verdienen.

29

29 M Summary ⚬⚬

Mr Grant works at home as an inventor. He has invented all kinds of clever machines, but he hasn't sold any of his inventions yet. One day he receives a visit from Dr Jane Egan from Western Gadgets Ltd. Mrs Egan is coming to look at some of his inventions, for example a special armchair and a remote-controlled drink bar. Mr Grant tries to make coffee for his guest, but the drink bar doesn't work too well. There isn't enough water in the machine. Jane suggests that he should improve the machine and that he could connect it to the tap, so there'd always be enough water in it. It is obvious that this inventor needs a better workshop. Mrs Egan feels he has talent and tells him to apply for a job with her firm. The inventor likes the idea until he hears that the boss is Jim Faraday. Mr Faraday used to be his physics teacher. Mr Grant is convinced Mr Faraday wouldn't want him. Physics was not Russell's best subject.

There's nothing like doing things by oneself

Vocabulary			Wortschatz
29	to invent	tʊ ɪn'vent	erfinden
	discovery	dɪ'skʌvərɪ	Entdeckung
	Industrial Revolution	ɪn'dʌstrɪəl revə'lu:ʃn	Industrielle Revolution
	steam-engine	'sti:m endʒɪn	Dampfmaschine
	locomotive	ləʊkə'məʊtɪv	Lokomotive
	textile industry	'tekstaɪl 'ɪndəstrɪ	Textilindustrie
	power-loom	'paʊə lu:m	Webstuhl
	spinning-machine	'spɪnɪŋ məʃi:n	Spinnmaschine
	to discover	tə dɪ'skʌvə	entdecken
	penicillin	penɪ'sɪlɪn	Penizillin
	to display	tə dɪ'spleɪ	ausstellen
	development	dɪ'veləpmənt	Entwicklung
	electronics	ɪlek'trɒnɪks	Elektronik
	space flight	'speɪs flaɪt	(Welt-)Raumflug
	photography	fə'tɒgrəfɪ	Photographie
	printing	'prɪntɪŋ	Buchdruckerkunst
	nuclear physics	'nju:klɪə 'fɪzɪks	Atomphysik
29 A	inventor	ɪn'ventə	Erfinder
	if it is convenient for you	kən'vi:njənt	wenn es Ihnen recht ist
	household	'haʊshəʊld	Haushalt
	gadget	'gædʒɪt	Apparat, Gerät
	yours sincerely	jɔ:z sn'sɪəlɪ	mit freundlichen Grüßen
	limited	'lɪmɪtɪd	beschränkt, begrenzt
	limited company (Ltd.)	'lɪmɪtɪd 'kʌmpənɪ	Gesellschaft mit beschränkter Haftung
	punctual	'pʌŋktʃʊəl	pünktlich
	to see s.b.	tə si:	jdn. treffen, besuchen
	armchair	ɑ:m'tʃeə, 'ɑ:mtʃeə	Arm-, Lehnstuhl
	anybody	'enɪbɒdɪ	(irgend)jemand
	to sit up	tə sɪt 'ʌp	aufrecht sitzen
	straight	streɪt	gerade
	to lie down	tə laɪ 'daʊn	sich hinlegen
	remote-controlled	rɪ'məʊt kən'trəʊld	ferngesteuert
	drink bar	'drɪŋk bɑ:	Getränkebar
	control panel	kən'trəʊl 'pænl	Armaturenbrett, Schaltbrett, Schalttafel
	to choose	tə 'tʃu:z	auswählen
	to connect	tə kə'nekt	verbinden, anschließen
	tap	tæp	(Wasser-)Hahn
	tip	tɪp	Hinweis, Tip
	to advise s.b. on s.th.	tʊ əd'vaɪz	jdn. bei etwas beraten
	to improve	tʊ ɪm'pru:v	verbessern
	to earn one's living	tʊ 'ɜ:n wʌnz 'lɪvɪŋ	seinen Lebensunterhalt verdienen

	library	'laɪbrərɪ	Bücherei, Bibliothek
	trained	treɪnd	ausgebildet
	librarian	laɪ'breərɪən	Bibliothekar(in)
	not exactly	nɒt ɪg'zæktlɪ	nicht ganz
	regular	'regjʊlə	regelmäßig
	a monthly salary	ə 'mʌnθlɪ 'sælərɪ	ein Monatsgehalt, ein monatliches Gehalt
	automatic	ɔ:tə'mætɪk	automatisch
	to turn over	tə tɜ:n 'əʊvə	umblättern
	page	peɪdʒ	Seite
	research and development department	rɪ'sɜ:tʃ ən dɪ'veləpmənt dɪpɑ:tmənt	Forschungs- und Entwicklungsabteilung
	dark	dɑ:k	dunkel(haarig)
	grammar school	'græmə sku:l	Gymnasium, höhere Schule
	former	'fɔ:mə	ehemalig, früher
	physics teacher	'fɪzɪks ti:tʃə	Physiklehrer
	forgetful	fə'gətfʊl	vergeßlich
29 B	amateur	'æmətə	Laie, Amateur
	none	nʌn	keine(-r, -s)
	situation	sɪtjʊ'eɪʃn	Lage, Position, Stellung
	physicist	'fɪzɪsɪst	Physiker
	field	fi:ld	Bereich, Sach-, Fachgebiet
	electricity	ɪlek'trɪsətɪ	Elektrizität(slehre)
	electromagnetics	ɪlektrəʊmæg'netɪks	Elektromagnetik
29 F	unless	ən'les	wenn nicht
	to pass a test	tə 'pɑ:s ə 'test	eine Prüfung, einen Test bestehen
29 H	president	'prezɪdənt	Präsident
	burglar	'bɜ:glə	Einbrecher
	double (adj.)	'dʌbl	doppelt
29 K	reason	'ri:zn	Grund, Ursache; Begründung
	to state	tə 'steɪt	darlegen, erklären, aussagen
29 M	to receive	tə rɪ'si:v	empfangen, erhalten, bekommen
	obvious	'ɒbvɪəs	offensichtlich, klar, deutlich
	talent	'tælənt	Begabung, Talent
	convinced	kən'vɪnst	überzeugt
	subject	'sʌbdʒɪkt, 'sʌbdʒekt	Fach

UNIT 30

Fleet Street in London

(CB) The British read a lot of newspapers. They read wherever they go: sitting in the Underground or in a bus or waiting in a queue.
Most newspapers have their head offices in Fleet Street. This street is full of life at night when the press people are at work.
Three of the daily papers are called quality papers: *The Times, The Daily Telegraph* and *The Guardian.* These papers cover and comment on important political news. There are also a number of popular papers: the *Daily Mirror,* the *Daily Express,* the *Daily Mail,* the *Daily Star,* and *The Sun.* These papers have a much larger circulation. Besides the daily papers there are several quality Sunday papers: *The Observer, The Sunday Times* and the *Sunday Telegraph.* Other Sunday papers like the *News of the World,* the *Sunday Mirror* and the *Sunday Express* are more sensational.
An interesting newspaper is the *Financial Times.* It is printed in London and Frankfurt and calls itself "Europe's Business Newspaper". However, it is not only a paper for business people, it also informs its readers about politics and new developments in technology, and contains reviews of plays, concerts, films and other cultural events.

30 A The editor's office

(J = Jane, R = Russell, E = Editor, L = Lynda, Fred Roberts' secretary)

J Why did I ever become a reporter?
R Don't ask me!
J I'll be working all day tomorrow again.
R Will you really?
R Hard luck, Jane!
I won't be working tomorrow.
J Won't you really?
R No, I won't.

R I'm taking a week off.
J You're always taking time off.
R No, I'm not.
I haven't had a holiday since . . .
J . . . your last holiday.

(enter editor)
E Russell, have you finished that article yet? The paper comes out in three hours.
R All right, Joe.
I'll have finished it by 11 o'clock.
E Okay. But I've got to have it by 11 o'clock at the latest.
R Do you like the headline?
MINISTER OF TRANSPORT OPENS NEW MOTORWAY
E That's all right. But hurry up a bit.
J Oh dear, I've got three stories to cover tomorrow.
I'll be working late again.
R Poor you!
This time tomorrow you'll be working.
And I'll be sitting on the terrace of my hotel, looking at the moonlight, listening to the sea . . .
J Where are you going?
R I'm going to Jersey for a week.
J Who'll be doing your work while you're away?
R Fred Roberts from the news desk.
He's been on holiday. He'll be coming back this evening.
He'll be doing my work till I get back.
J But he doesn't know anything about politics! He'll be asking me questions all the time!

(enter editor again)
E What? Still chatting?
When are you going to do some work?
R Don't worry, I'll have finished it by eleven.
E We can't finish the front page until we've got your article.

30

R Okay, okay.
J So you're going away during the conference?
R That's right! But Fred'll be covering it, so it'll be all right.
Oh – I must remember to get my camera back from him before I go.
He wanted to have it till tomorrow evening, but I've got to have it back by tomorrow morning – my plane takes off at lunchtime.
I must phone him.

(R phones Fred Roberts' office)
L Hello. Fred Roberts' office.
R Hello, Lynda – Russell here.
Can I speak to Fred?
L He's not here . . . he's . . .
(Russell interrupts her)
R Oh well, I just wanted to give him some details about the Foreign Secretary's visit. He'll be arriving here at about 12.30 tomorrow. He'll be coming in his official car of course.
L I've been trying to tell you he's got flu.
The doctor says he'll be staying in bed for at least two weeks.
R You're joking.
L No, I'm afraid it's true.
R Well, that's the end of my holiday.

(enter editor)

E Russell, there's something I've got to tell you.

R I know – Fred Roberts is ill.

E Yes, I'm awfully sorry, but you'll just have to put off your holiday till some other time.

R But this is my first week off since . . .

E I'm sure we can find another time for you. It can't be helped. The paper comes first.

R Can't Jack do it?

E I'm afraid not.
He's had an accident.
He won't be coming in for a while.
Now you'll be covering the conference tomorrow and you'll be taking over Fred's work at the news desk as well.
So you'll be spending next week in Manchester. The Federation of British Engineers is having its annual conference from Monday to Friday next week.
You'll be very busy.
By this time tomorrow you'll have forgotten all about your holidays!

R I bet I will have done.

(E goes off)

R Why did I ever become a reporter?

J Don't ask me.
Cheer up, Russell!
I'll send you a postcard.

R Where from?

J From Jersey.
I'll be going there next Sunday.
I'm covering the Jersey Flower Show.
I'll be thinking of you while you're in Manchester!

30 B Questions

What sort of paper would you call *The Daily Telegraph*?
What is a popular paper?
Which Sunday "sister" papers do you know?
Which paper has got a larger circulation – *The Times* or the *Daily Mirror*?
Is the *Financial Times* only for business people?
Why can't Russell take the holiday he wanted?
What'll Russell be doing next week?
What is Jane going to do in Jersey?

30 C And you?

Do you read an English newspaper or magazine sometimes?
Which part of a newspaper do you like best, and why?

30 D Future Continuous — Verlaufsform der Zukunft

I'll be working late.	*Ich werde bis spät in die Nacht arbeiten.*
I won't be working tomorrow.	*Ich werde morgen nicht arbeiten.*

Die Verlaufsform der Zukunft wird mit **"will (shall)" + be + ing-Form des Verbs** gebildet.

30 E Use of the Future Continuous — Verwendung der Verlaufsform der Zukunft

This time tomorrow I'll be sitting on the terrace of my hotel.	*Morgen um diese Zeit werde ich auf der Terrasse meines Hotels sitzen.*
The Foreign Secretary will be coming in his official car.	*Der Außenminister wird in seinem Dienstwagen kommen.*
Will you be coming tonight?	*Werden Sie heute abend kommen?*

30

Die Verlaufsform der Zukunft schildert Handlungen, die sich zu einem bestimmten Zeitpunkt in der Zukunft ereignen werden.
Sie steht auch für Handlungen, die voraussichtlich, im normalen Ablauf der Dinge, in der Zukunft eintreten werden.
Fragen nach den künftigen Handlungen anderer Personen wirken durch die Verwendung des Future Continuous besonders behutsam und höflich. In vielen Fällen kann man das Future Continuous durch das Present Continuous ersetzen: When will you be coming back? / When are you coming back? Will you be coming tonight? / Are you coming tonight?

30 F Setzen Sie das Verb in die Verlaufsform der Zukunft. Verwenden Sie dabei, wo dies nötig ist, Zeitangaben wie z. B. tomorrow, next week etc. ○○

I was working yesterday.
I was working hard this time last week.
Fred was covering the story.
She saw him last Friday.
We went to the cinema last night.
He came by train.
I visited my friends in the States last year.
He took a week off.
I was sitting on the beach this time last week.
I was thinking of you.

30 G Put the sentences into the Future Continuous: ○○

When are you leaving?
Who are you going with?
Are you travelling by plane?
Aren't you taking the children?
Where are you staying?
What day are you coming back?
Why aren't you staying longer?

30 H Future Perfect — Vollendete Zukunft

He'll have finished the article by 11 o'clock.	*Er wird den Artikel bis 11 Uhr beendet (geschrieben) haben.*

Die vollendete Zukunft wird mit **"will (shall)"** und der **Perfektform des Verbs** (vgl. Bd. 2, Unit 21) gebildet.
Diese Form ist teils Zukunft, teils Perfekt. Wir verwenden sie, wenn eine Handlung zu einem bestimmten Zeitpunkt der Zukunft vorbei sein, abgeschlossen sein wird. Der Zeitpunkt wird sehr häufig durch die Präposition "by" angegeben: by 11 o'clock, *bis 11 Uhr;* by tomorrow, *bis morgen.*

30 I Complete the sentences with the Future Perfect: OO

I . . . . (to pay) for the car by the end of the year.
You . . . . (to start) your holidays this time next week, won't you?
The minister . . . . (to open) the motorway by midday.
Russell . . . . (to learn) a lot about engineering after his visit to Manchester.
I . . . . (not, to make) my decision until tomorrow evening.

30 J till / until – by

We'll be sending you the Financial Times **till (until)** the end of March.	*Wir werden Ihnen die Financial Times bis einschließlich Ende März zuschicken.*
Please pay **by** the end of March.	*Bitte bezahlen Sie bis Ende März.*

Wenn etwas ununterbrochen, ständig geschieht (die Zeitung wird jeden Tag geliefert) verwendet man "till" bzw. "until".
"By" dagegen steht, wenn etwas nur einmal zu einem bestimmten Zeitpunkt erfolgt (das Zeitungsabonnement wird nicht ununterbrochen, sondern nur einmal bezahlt).

30 K Complete the sentences with "till" ("until") or "by": OO

I'll lend you the money . . . . . next week.
Can you return it . . . . . next week?
The guests stayed . . . . 10 o'clock.
Please send us your application . . . . . 15 January.
We'll be staying in London . . . . . Christmas.
He's on holiday . . . . . 25 August.

30 L

TIMES PAST

THE TIMES

P.O. Box 7, 200 Gray's Inn Road, London WC1X 8EZ. Telephone: 01-837 1234

A letter to the editor

Dear Sir,

I really must protest at the announcement that the government spent £300 million last year in aid to the developing countries. With our own pensioners going cold in the winter I consider it monstrous. Charity begins at home.

Yours faithfully,
Lane Blackwell

30 M *Write a letter to the editor either agreeing or disagreeing with the letter above.*

30 N Situation – Say it in English

Fragen Sie Ihre Freundin, wann sie mit ihrer Arbeit fertig sein wird.
Ihre Freundin antwortet, daß sie bis morgen abend fertig sein wird.
Sagen Sie, daß Sie nächste Woche in London sein werden. (= verbringen werden)
Sie arbeiten in einer Zeitungsredaktion. Ein Anrufer möchte den Chefredakteur sprechen.
Erklären Sie dem Anrufer, daß der Chefredakteur leider nicht da ist.
Sagen Sie, daß er am Nachmittag kommen wird.
Sagen Sie, daß Sie morgen um diese Zeit nach New York fliegen werden (...auf dem Flug nach New York sein werden).
Sagen Sie, daß Sie eine Woche dort bleiben werden.

Meet the Press

30 O Summary

Russell and Jane are newspaper reporters. They work in the same office. Russell is in a good mood. He's going on holiday and while Jane is working, he'll be relaxing in Jersey. While they are talking, the editor comes in to get an article from Russell. He needs it quickly. Russell promises him that he'll have finished it by eleven o'clock.

Suddenly Russell remembers that he must phone Fred Roberts to get his camera back. Fred will be doing Russell's work for a week. But Russell gets a nasty shock when he hears that Fred has got flu and will be staying in bed for two weeks. That puts a sudden end to Russell's holiday plans. He won't be sitting on a hotel terrace tomorrow after all; he'll be working. The editor comes in to tell Russell that he must go to Manchester to write about the engineering conference. He'll be doing Fred's work as well as his own, so Russell will soon have forgotten all about holidays! While Russell is reporting from Manchester, Jane will be going to Jersey. She's covering the Jersey Flower Show.

Vocabulary			Wortschatz
30	wherever	weər'evə	wo(hin) auch immer, ganz gleich, wo(hin)
	head office	hed 'ɒfɪs	Hauptsitz, Hauptbüro, Zentrale
	at night	ət 'naɪt	nachts, abends
	press people	'pres pi:pl	Zeitungsleute
	to be at work	tə bɪ ət 'wɜ:k	arbeiten
	daily paper	'deɪlɪ peɪpə	Tageszeitung
	quality	'kwɒlətɪ	Qualität, Güte
	to cover s.th.	tə 'kʌvə	etwas behandeln, über etwas berichten; etwas enthalten, beinhalten
	to comment on s.th.	tə kɒment 'ɒn	etwas kommentieren, erläutern
	political	pə'lɪtɪkl	politisch
	circulation	sɜ:kjʊ'leɪʃn	Auflage(nhöhe)
	besides	bɪ'saɪdz	neben, außer
	Sunday paper	'sʌndɪ peɪpə	Sonntagszeitung
	sensational	sen'seɪʃnəl	aufsehenerregend, auf Effekthascherei bedacht, sensationell
	to print	tə 'prɪnt	drucken
	business people	'bɪznɪs pi:pl	Geschäftsleute
	to inform	tʊ ɪn'fɔ:m	informieren
	reader	'ri:də	Leser
	politics	'pɒlɪtɪks	Politik
	technology	tek'nɒlədʒɪ	angewandte Naturwissenschaft, Technologie
	to contain	tə kən'teɪn	enthalten
	review	rɪ'vju:	Besprechung, Kritik, Rezension
	cultural	'kʌltʃərəl	kulturell, Kultur-
	event	ɪ'vent	Ereignis, Begebenheit
30 A	editor	'edɪtə	Herausgeber, Schriftleiter, (Chef-)Redakteur
	Hard luck!	hɑ:d 'lʌk	So ein Pech!
	to take time off	tə 'teɪk 'taɪm ɒf	sich freinehmen, Urlaub machen
	to come out	tə kʌm 'aʊt	herauskommen, erscheinen *(Zeitung, Buch etc.)*
	headline	'hedlaɪn	Schlagzeile
	Minister of Transport	'mɪnɪstər əv 'trɑ:nspɔ:t, 'trænspɔ:t	Verkehrsminister(in)
	Poor you!	'pɔ: 'ju:	Du Arme(r)!
	terrace	'terəs	Terrasse
	moonlight	'mu:nlaɪt	Mondschein
	sea	si:	Meer
	news desk	'nju:z desk	Nachrichtenredaktion

	till	tɪl	bis
	front page	'frʌnt 'peɪdʒ	Titelseite
	camera	'kæmrə	Kamera, Fotoapparat
	to take off	tə teɪk 'ɒf	abfliegen, starten
	at lunchtime	ət 'lʌntʃtaɪm	mittags, um die Mittagszeit
	to interrupt	tʊ ɪntə'rʌpt	unterbrechen
	Foreign Secretary	'fɒrən 'sekrətrɪ	Außenminister(in)
	flu	flu:	Grippe
	to joke	tə 'dʒəʊk	scherzen, Witze machen
	to put off	tə pʊt 'ɒf	auf-, verschieben
	for a while	fər ə 'waɪl	eine Weile
	to take over	tə teɪk 'əʊvə	übernehmen
	federation	fedə'reɪʃn	Vereinigung, Verband
	to bet	tə 'bet	einer Sache sicher sein, wetten
	Cheer up!	tʃɪər 'ʌp	Kopf hoch!
	show	ʃəʊ	Ausstellung
30 B	picture	'pɪktʃə	Bild
	space	speɪs	Platz, Raum
	to report (of, on)	tə rɪ'pɔ:t (ɒv, ɒn)	berichten (über)
	scientific	saɪən'tɪfɪk	(natur)wissenschaftlich
	information	ɪnfə'meɪʃn	Information, Nachricht
	to be unable	tə bɪ ʌn'eɪbl	unfähig sein, nicht in der Lage sein
30 C	magazine	mægə'zi:n	Zeitschrift
30 F	beach	bi:tʃ	Strand
30 I	midday	'mɪddeɪ	Mittag
	to learn	tə 'lɜ:n	lernen
30 L	to protest	tə prə'test	protestieren, Einspruch erheben
	announcement	ə'naʊnsmənt	Ankündigung
	to spend	tə 'spend	ausgeben
	aid	eɪd	Hilfe(leistung), Unterstützung
	developing countries	dɪ'veləpɪŋ 'kʌntrɪz	Entwicklungsländer
	pensioner	'penʃənə	Pensionär(in)
	to consider	tə kən'sɪdə	betrachten
	monstrous	'mɒnstrəs	ungeheuerlich, absurd
	charity	'tʃærətɪ	Nächstenliebe
30 M	either	'aɪðə	entweder
	to disagree	tə dɪsə'gri:	nicht übereinstimmen, nicht einer Meinung sein
	published	'pʌblɪʃt	veröffentlicht
30 O	in a good mood	ɪn ə gʊd 'mu:d	in guter Stimmung, Laune
	to relax	tə rɪ'læks	entspannen
	nasty	'nɑ:stɪ	böse, schlimm
	shock	ʃɒk	Schock, Schreck
	sudden	'sʌdn	plötzlich, überraschend, unvermutet

UNIT 31

The Houses of Parliament in Westminster

31

CB Great Britain is a parliamentary democracy. The Parliament in Westminster is in fact the oldest in the world and is often called the "Mother of Parliaments". Parliament consists of the House of Commons and the House of Lords.
The real power lies with the House of Commons. The people elect its 650 members in a general election every four or five years. Each member represents one of the over six hundred constituencies. There are no party lists. If a candidate doesn't win in his constituency, then he cannot become an MP. This system is known as the majority vote system.

31 A The election campaign

(J = Jane, R = Russell, C 1 = Candidate 1, C 2 = Candidate 2)

C 1 Good morning! May I have a word with you?
J What did you say?
C 1 May I come in?
J Oh come in – I can't hear a word you're saying.
C 1 What a noise! That's better.
C 1 May I introduce myself? I'm Jack Brown, your Labour candidate. Could you spare me a few moments?
J Well, I'm rather busy – what do you want?
C 1 Do you mind if I ask you a few questions?

J Well, all right.
C 1 Who did you vote for at the last election?
J I didn't vote last time – I was too young.
C 1 Ah. If you had voted, you would have voted for us. Am I right?
J Well, actually I don't think so.
C 1 Why not, if I may ask?
J Well, you built this busy road right in front of our house.
If you hadn't built it, it wouldn't be so noisy here.
C 1 We didn't build it, madam, that was the Conservatives.
If we had been in government, that wouldn't have happened.

(R in overalls, mending television set)
R What would you have done if you'd been in power last time?
C 1 We would have, er . . . built the road along the other side of the park.
R But there's a school and lots of houses over there as well!
C 1 Ah, but we would have built more schools for your children.
J But I haven't got any children.
C 1 But who did you vote for last time?

The Speaker's Procession

R I didn't vote for your party.
But what will you do if you win this time?
C 1 We're going to keep prices down and incomes up. If we had been in government last time, there wouldn't have been such a rise in the cost of living.
J But if you put incomes up, prices will go up as well.
C 1 Well, you can take it from me, madam, that if you vote for us, you'll spend less on shopping and you'll have more money in your purse. So don't forget: "BROWN FOR THIS TOWN."
J Well, thank you. Goodbye.
C 1 Goodbye.

R It would be a mistake if you voted for him.
J Why?
R You don't believe all he says, do you?
J Well, he's a very nice man, isn't he?
R They're all very nice. But that's not enough.
It's action we want, not words.
If they did more and talked less, we'd all be happier.
(doorbell again)
J Oh, good morning . . .
C 2 May I come in? Thank you.
It's so noisy out here.
I won't keep you a moment.
Oh, er . . . may I introduce myself?
My name's Jeremy Swallow.
I'm your Conservative candidate.
If we had been in government for another six months, we would have stopped the traffic in this road.
R But you were in government for five years!
C 2 Yes, indeed, sir. But that wasn't long enough.
R And what would you have done about the traffic in this road?

C 2 We would have built another road along the other side of the park.
J But your party wanted this road – right in front of our house!
C 2 Oh no, that wasn't our party. That was your local authority, madam, and they're all from the Labour Party.
If more people had voted for us at the last local elections, you wouldn't have had the road here at all!
R That's what they all say.
J What else will you do if you're elected?
C 2 We'll put incomes up and keep prices down and we'll reduce income tax for young families . . .
R So you'll do all that if you get in?
C 2 Yes, of course we will.
We Conservatives always keep our word.
Did the country go to ruin while we were in government?
J Well, . . .
C 2 There you are! You see – we saved the country from ruin.
R If they'd been in government any longer, they'd have ruined the country completely!
C 2 So don't forget, madam:
"FOLLOW SWALLOW."

J What a charming man, don't you agree?
R Not really, Mrs Egan.
These politicians! They all say the same.
If I were you, I wouldn't vote for either of them.
J Why not?
R They've been in government long enough. What we want is a change.
R If you vote for them, we'll never get out of our difficulties.
J What difficulties do you mean?
R Prices are going up, incomes are going down. They're ruining the country.
J Then who do you think I should vote for?
R For the young party, the Social Democrats. They're going to tackle the real problems and really improve things for everyone.
J But I've never seen their candidate.
R Yes, you have, madam –
"ACTION – NOT WORDS." That's our motto.
I'm the Social Democrat candidate.
I hope you'll vote for me!
J Well, thank you – very interesting . . .
J I'm not going to vote for any of you. My brother's the Independent candidate, and if I didn't vote for him, it would probably be unfair, wouldn't it?

31

31 B Questions

What is the British Parliament sometimes called? Why?
How often do the British people elect a new parliament?
In what way does a party candidate become a Member of Parliament?
Why didn't Jane vote last time?
What are the candidates in our story doing to win votes in their constituency?

31 C And you?

What are the main political parties in your country?
When was the last election in your country?
Which party got the most votes at that election?

31 D Conditional clauses (II) — Bedingungssätze

Type 3

if-clause: had + past participle	main clause: would have + past participle
If **you had voted,** *Wenn Sie gewählt hätten,*	**you would have voted** for us. *hätten Sie uns Ihre Stimme gegeben.*
If **we'd been** in government for another six months, *Wenn wir noch weitere sechs Monate regiert hätten,*	**we would have stopped** the traffic in this road. *hätten wir den Verkehr in dieser Straße gestoppt.*

Wenn die Bedingung nicht verwirklicht wurde, also nicht mehr möglich ist, verwenden wir Typ 3: im if-Satz "had" mit dem Partizip Perfekt, im Hauptsatz "would (bzw. "could" oder "might") have" mit dem Partizip Perfekt.

31 E Complete the sentences:

If he had parked the car somewhere else, he . . . . a ticket. (not get)
If Russell . . . . in the 18th century, he would have invented the steam-engine. (live)
If they . . . . enough money, they wouldn't have robbed the bank. (have)
If I . . . . time, I would read the paper. (have)
If the weather . . . . fine, I would go for a walk. (be)
If she hadn't won the football pools, she . . . . this car. (not buy)
If I had the money, I . . . . round the world. (go)
If he had been more careful, he . . . . himself. (not hurt)
Russell . . . . if you don't invite him. (not come)
He could have helped us if he . . . . to. (want)

31 F What would you have done if . . . . . ?

- you had won £50,000 on the football pools?
- you had missed the plane?
- you had failed your driving test?
- the car park had been full?
- your car had broken down on the motorway?
- you had had time this afternoon?

31 G Unreal Past Tense **Irreale Vergangenheitsform**

If only I knew what you wanted.	*Wenn ich nur wüßte, was du willst.*
If only he had some experience.	*Wenn er nur etwas Erfahrung hätte.*

Die irreale Vergangenheitsform (der irreale Bedingungssatz) kann auch für sich allein stehen. Er drückt einen Wunsch aus, dessen Erfüllung mehr als fraglich ist.

31

31 H Put in the missing words: (CB) ○○

Every four or five years the British people . . . . in a general election. This election decides who is going to represent the people in the House of . . . .
There are no elections for the House of . . . .
Many people think that the majority . . . . system is not fair. In Germany, if a candidate doesn't win a . . . ., he or she has still won some votes for his or her . . . . and may get into Parliament through the party . . . . In Britain these . . . . . are lost.

31 I Discussion

Compare the majority vote system with the election system in your country.
Suggest two matters of public interest that should be discussed in the Parliament of your country.

31 J *Write a letter to a friend of yours in Britain or in the United States. Say what in your opinion is the most important problem today (e. g. unemployment, nuclear war, inflation, crime, hunger, etc.).*

31 K Situation – Say it in English

Sie werden gefragt, wie es Ihnen zur Zeit geht.
Antworten Sie, daß es Ihnen ganz gut geht.
Sagen Sie, daß es schlechter sein könnte.
Ihr Gesprächspartner fragt Sie, ob Sie etwas dagegen haben, wenn er Ihnen ein paar Fragen stellt.

Ihr Gesprächspartner versichert, daß er Sie nicht lange aufhalten wird.
Antworten Sie, daß Sie nichts dagegen haben.
Sagen Sie, daß Sie anderer Meinung sind.

31 L Summary ○○

It was election time again and all the candidates were going from house to house to ask people to vote for their party. Russell was doing some work at Jane's house when the Labour candidate arrived. Jane asked him what his party would have done if they had won the last election and what they would do if they won this one. He replied they wouldn't have built the noisy road outside Jane's house and that they would keep prices down and put incomes up. Jane thought he was a nice man but Russell was not convinced. He thought people would be better off if politicians talked less and did more work.

Jane thought the Conservative candidate was just charming. He also promised that his party would keep prices down and put incomes up. Russell didn't agree. He said the Conservatives would have ruined the country completely if they had stayed in government. In Russell's opinion people should vote for the Social Democrats. It finally came out that he himself was their candidate. But Jane wouldn't vote for any of these candidates because her brother was the Independent candidate and she was going to vote for him.

I'll keep my word

Vocabulary			Wortschatz
31	parliamentary	pɑːləˈmentərɪ	parlamentarisch
	democracy	dɪˈmɒkrəsɪ	Demokratie
	House of Commons	ˈhaʊs əv ˈkɒmənz	Unterhaus
	House of Lords	ˈhaʊs əv ˈlɔːdz	Oberhaus
	to lie with	tə ˈlaɪ wɪð	liegen bei
	to elect	tʊ ɪˈlekt	wählen
	general election	ˈdʒenrəl ɪˈlekʃn	Parlamentswahl
	to represent	tə reprɪˈzent	(einen Wahlkreis) vertreten
	constituency	kənˈstɪtjʊənsɪ	Wahlkreis, Wahlbezirk
	party list	pɑːtɪ ˈlɪst	Parteiliste
	candidate	ˈkændɪdeɪt, ~dɪt, ~dət	Kandidat(in), Bewerber(in)
	Member of Parliament	ˈmembər əv ˈpɑːləmənt	Abgeordnete(r) (des Unterhauses)
	majority vote system	məˈdʒɒrətɪ ˈvəʊt sɪstəm	Mehrheitswahlsystem
31 A	election campaign	ɪˈlekʃn kæmpeɪn	Wahlkampf, Wahlfeldzug
	Labour	ˈleɪbə	die Labour Party
	to spare	tə ˈspeə	erübrigen
	to vote for s.b.	tə ˈvəʊt fə sʌmbədɪ	für jdn. stimmen
	in front of	ɪn ˈfrʌnt ɒv	vor (räumlich)
	Conservative	kənˈsɜːvətɪv	die Konservative Partei
	overalls	ˈəʊvərɔːlz	Arbeits-, Monteuranzug
	side	saɪd	Seite
	to keep down	tə kiːp ˈdaʊn	niedrig halten
	income	ˈɪnkʌm	Einkommen
	to keep up	tə kiːp ˈʌp	hochhalten
	rise	raɪz	Erhöhung
	the cost of living	ðə ˈkɒst əv ˈlɪvɪŋ	die Lebenshaltungskosten
	to put up	tə pʊt ˈʌp	erhöhen
	to go up	tə gəʊ ˈʌp	ansteigen
	purse	pɜːs	Geldbeutel, Brieftasche
	action	ˈækʃn	Tat(en)
	I won't keep you a moment	aɪ ˈwəʊnt kiːp jʊ ə ˈməʊmənt	ich werde Sie nicht lange aufhalten
	local authority	ˈləʊkl ɔːˈθɒrətɪ	Ortsbehörde, Gemeindeamt
	local elections	ˈləʊkl ɪˈlekʃnz	Kommunal-, Gemeindewahlen
	to reduce	tə rɪˈdjuːs	verringern
	income tax	ˈɪnkəm tæks	Einkommensteuer
	to get in (power)	tə get ˈɪn	an die Macht kommen, gelangen
	ruin	ˈrʊɪn	Untergang, Ruin
	to ruin	tə ˈrʊɪn	ruinieren
	to save	tə ˈseɪv	retten, bewahren
	completely	kəmˈpliːtlɪ	vollständig
	politician	pɒlɪˈtɪʃn	Politiker

31

	I wouldn't vote for either of them	aɪ 'wʊdnt vəʊt fər 'aɪðər əv ðəm	ich würde keinen von ihnen wählen
	change	tʃeɪndʒ	Veränderung
	to get out of s.th.	tə get 'aʊt əv sʌmθɪŋ	aus etwas herauskommen
	difficulty	'dɪfɪkəltɪ	Schwierigkeit
	Social Democrat	'səʊʃl 'deməkræt	Sozialdemokrat(in); sozialdemokratisch
	to tackle a problem	tə 'tækl ə 'prɒbləm	ein Problem in Angriff nehmen, anpacken, angehen, lösen
	motto	'mɒtəʊ	Motto, Wahlspruch
	unfair	ʌn'feə	ungerecht, unfair
31 B	voter	'vəʊtə	Wähler
31 C	main	meɪn	hauptsächlich, vorwiegend, Haupt-
31 E	to rob	tə 'rɒb	(be)rauben, stehlen
	to go for a walk	tə 'gəʊ fər ə wɔːk	einen Spaziergang machen
31 F	owner-occupied flat	'əʊnər ɒkjʊpaɪd 'flæt	Eigentumswohnung
	to fail a test	tə 'feɪl ə 'test	eine Prüfung nicht bestehen
	breakdown service	'breɪkdaʊn sɜːvɪs	Pannendienst
31 H	fair	feə	gerecht, anständig
31 I	matter	'mætə	Angelegenheit, Sache
	public	'pʌblɪk	öffentlich
	to discuss	tə dɪ'skʌs	diskutieren, erörtern
31 J	unemployment	ʌnɪm'plɔɪmənt	Arbeitslosigkeit
	nuclear war	'njuːklɪə 'wɔː	Atomkrieg
	inflation	ɪn'fleɪʃn	Inflation
	crime	kraɪm	Verbrechen
	hunger	'hʌŋgə	Hunger
31 L	to reply	tə rɪ'plaɪ	antworten, erwidern
	to promise	tə 'prɒmɪs	versprechen

UNIT 32

A farm house in Britain

32

CB Neighbours play an important part in most people's lives. Friendly, helpful neighbours make life easier and more pleasant, while unfriendly neighbours can be a real problem. In the suburbs of most British towns, where people live in detached or semi-detached houses and have their own gardens, chatting to the neighbours over the garden fence is a popular activity, especially at weekends. But in city centres or in modern high-rise blocks of flats, people often have no contact with their neighbours and feel lonely and lost.

32 A The helpful neighbour

(J = Jane, R = Russell)

J Oh, that dripping tap!
It's driving me mad!
It's been dripping for weeks now.
I ought to mend it, but I don't know how.
Anyway, somebody has got to mend it.
Ah, there's Mr Grant in his garden.
Perhaps he can mend it.
I'll ask him.
Hello, Mr Grant.

R Good morning, Mrs Egan.
Nice weather we're having.

J Yes, isn't it lovely?
We've been very lucky with the weather so far this summer.

R Yes, we have, haven't we?
Your roses are beautiful this year.

J Thank you. I think I ought to cut them back a bit.
Your wife's very lucky, isn't she?

J You do everything around the house.
R Well, not everything.
Look, I'm not allowed to cut down that old tree over there.
J But your wife's right. Old trees are wonderful.
You shouldn't cut it down.
By the way, could I ask you a favour?
R Yes, of course. What is it?
J Do you know anyone who can mend taps?
R Why do you ask?
J Because the tap in my kitchen drips.
It's been dripping for months.
I ought to have mended it a long time ago.
R Well, it's not difficult to mend taps.
I've mended hundreds of them.
In fact I had to mend one only yesterday. There's nothing to it.
J I've just got to get someone to mend my tap. I can't stand it any longer.
R You needn't get anybody.
I'll mend it for you.
J Oh, you don't have to do that – I didn't mean that!
R Nonsense. It's no trouble at all.
I won't be a minute.
I've just got to get my tools.
J It's nice to have such a helpful neighbour.

An English country church

J Come in, Mr Grant.
R Now where's that tap?
J There it is.
R Hm. Yes. That ought to be quite easy.
I'll be able to mend this all right.
Now where's my wrench?
It ought to be in the toolbox.
J Shall I put the toolbox on the table?
R No, no, it's too heavy.
You won't be able to lift it.
J Yes, I will. I'm quite strong.
I used to play hockey at school.
R It must be in here somewhere.
J Here it is.
R That is not a wrench. This is a pair of pliers. This is a wrench.
J I must watch you.
If you show me how to do it, I'll be able to do it myself in future.
R Right. Now watch carefully.
First of all you've got to take this off.
Hm. This is more difficult than I thought.
J Can I help you?
R No, you can't. But I need a rag.
May I use this one?
J No, I'm awfully sorry, that's the tea-towel. Use this.
R This is difficult.
I didn't have to work so hard yesterday.
I only had to take the top off and that was that.

J Shall I call the plumber?
R No, no.
You don't have to call the plumber.
I'll be able to mend it.
There! It ought to be all right now.
What's the bucket for?
J Perhaps we'll need it.
R No, we won't need it.
Phew! I'll have to take my jacket off.
Now it's coming.

J It takes a lot of strength.
R I used to play rugby at school.
J I'm so grateful for your help. I wouldn't have been able to do it by myself.
R Don't mention it. Just one more turn… Now it's coming. (The tap breaks and water goes all over the place.)
J Oh dear.
R Quick, where's that bucket?
J You should have turned the water off!
R I'm afraid you *will* have to call the plumber after all.
J Are you sure I'm allowed to ring him now?

32 B Questions

What's Russell doing at the beginning of the story?
What's Russell going to repair?
What must Russell get before he can repair it?
How would you characterise Russell?
What game did Jane use to play at school?
Whose job is it to mend taps?

32

32 C And you?

What can you repair by yourself?
Have you ever helped a neighbour of yours?
Do you have much contact with your neighbours?
Would you like to share the housework with your wife / husband?

32 D Auxiliaries (III) — Hilfsverben (III)

Die unvollständigen Hilfsverben

can – may – must – need – shall – will – used to – ought to

haben folgendes gemeinsam:
Sie nehmen in der 3. Person Singular nie ein -s an.
(He can speak English. She must go home.)
Frage und Verneinung, Kurzantwort und Frageanhängsel werden ohne "do" gebildet.
(Can I help you? We mustn't be late.)
Der Infinitiv wird ohne "to" angeschlossen. Ausnahme: "ought to" und "used to".

a) must / have to / needn't

	+	–
Present	must have (got) to, has (got) to	needn't don't have to, doesn't have to
Past	– – – had to	– – – didn't have to
Future	– – – will have to	– – – won't have to

"Must" kommt nur in der Gegenwart vor. Wenn wir andere Zeitstufen bilden wollen, verwenden wir die Ersatzform "have to" bzw. "have got to".
Mit "mustn't" drücken wir ein Verbot aus oder einen dringenden Rat, etwas nicht zu tun. "Mustn't" heißt also *nicht dürfen.* Liegt dagegen kein Zwang vor, verneinen wir mit "needn't", *nicht müssen, nicht brauchen.*
You needn't get anybody. (I can do it myself.)
You mustn't forget to answer the letter. (He is waiting for it.)

b) can / to be able to

	+	–
Present	can am, are, is able to	can't am, are, isn't able to
Past	could was, were able to	couldn't was, weren't able to
Future	– – – will be able to	– – – won't be able to

Auch "can" ist unvollständig. Es gibt die Gegenwartsform "can" und die Vergangenheitsform "could". Die Ersatzform ist "to be able to", *imstande sein, gelingen.*
"Can" bedeutet *können,* also die physische oder geistige Fähigkeit, etwas zu tun. (I can lift the toolbox. I can speak English.) Ferner bedeutet es *dürfen, die Erlaubnis haben.* In diesem Fall hat "can" die gleiche Bedeutung wie "may". (Can I help you?)
"Could" bedeutet *könnte* (Could I come at five?) und *konnte* (I couldn't phone at five because your line was engaged.) Häufig nimmt man "to be able to" für *können.* (I wasn't able to phone at five.)

c) may / to be allowed to

Present	he may (not)	he is (not) allowed to
Past	– – –	he was (not) allowed to
Future	– – –	he will (won't) be allowed to

"May" drückt eine Erlaubnis aus. Mit der Ersatzform "to be allowed to" können wir alle Zeiten bilden.

d) ought to / should

I ought to	mend the tap.	*sollte, sollte eigentlich*
I should	mend the tap.	
I ought to	have mended it.	*hätte sollen*
I should	have mended it.	

"Ought to" drückt eine Verpflichtung oder einen Rat aus. Anstelle von "ought to" kann man auch "should" sagen. That should interest you. *Das dürfte Sie interessieren.*
Bei diesen "auxiliaries" ist die deutsche Entsprechung, die wir Ihnen geben, oft nur eine annähernde Beschreibung der genauen Bedeutung. Es sind keine Bedeutungsgleichungen. Beispiele: You can't stop there. *Du kannst (darfst) da nicht anhalten.* That should be all right. *Das dürfte in Ordnung sein.* He must be an expert. *Er ist bestimmt ein Fachmann.*

32

e) used to

Jane used to play hockey at school.

"Used to" drückt etwas aus, das in der Vergangenheit ständig oder häufig so war. Im Deutschen nimmt man für solche Aussagen meist Adverbien wie *früher, damals.*

32 E Complete the sentences with "can", "must", "may", "ought", "should", "shouldn't": QO

Anyone . . . . . learn English if he tries hard enough.
In England you . . . . . drive on the left.
It . . . . . rain tonight, but I hope it won't.
We . . . . . change our clothes for dinner.
You . . . . . to have called the plumber.
. . . . . I smoke here?
. . . . . you play the violin?
Customers . . . . . to count their change.
Women . . . . . earn the same money as men if they do the same job.
If you want to buy a house, you . . . . spend too much money on travelling.

32 F Translate the following sentences:

Sie hätte den Installateur rufen sollen.
Er hätte den Reifen wechseln sollen.
Wir würden uns freuen, wenn Ihr kommen könntet.
Er durfte das Handtuch nicht benützen.
Muß er über das Ingenieurstreffen berichten?
Sie müssen nicht unbedingt pünktlich sein. (2. Pers.)
Ich werde nicht kommen können.

32 G Put the following sentences into the past: ○○

I must say goodbye.
He needn't mend it.
We must discuss it again.
She needn't do it herself.
It must have a garden.
They needn't worry about it.
It must be good.

32 H Vocabulary practice

What do you call
- the time when a lot of people travel to or from work?
- a friendly welcome to guests?
- a person who repairs taps?
- a person living next door?
- the extra money you give to a waiter for good service?
- a person's family name?
- a man in prison?
- a man at the airport who wants to see what's in your luggage?

32 I Phonetics

Write the words in columns under the phonetic symbols: ○○

/e/	/iː/	/æ/	/ɑː/	/ɔː/	/ɒ/	/ʌ/

mean – stand – can't – long – enough – plumber – pleasant – ready – please – weather – sorry – cover – call – tap – piano – believe – cost – story – ask – trouble – job – what

32 J **An invitation**

Dear Graham,

Jane and I are holding a little housewarming party on Friday 5th February, and we would be glad if you could manage to come.
It is a very informal affair, just a few friends, so there will be no need to dress up.
Dinner will be around half past eight, but if you could come about half an hour earlier it will give us time for a chat and a drink.
We should be very pleased if you could join us.

Yours sincerely,

Jane and Russell

32 K *Invite a friend of yours to a barbecue.*

32 L **Situation - Say it in English**

Sagen Sie, daß Sie früher einmal Tennis gespielt haben.
Bitten Sie jemanden um einen Gefallen.
Bitten Sie jemanden, die Türe zu schließen.
Fragen Sie Ihren Nachbarn, ob er unbedingt hier rauchen muß.
Fragen Sie Ihren Gesprächspartner, ob er er wirklich meint, daß er die Polizei rufen sollte.
Sagen Sie, daß er recht haben mag.
Laden Sie jemanden zum Mittagessen ein.
Ihr Gesprächspartner findet das (die Einladung) großartig.

32

32 M **Summary** ꝏ

Jane had a problem last week. Her tap was dripping and it was driving her mad, but she couldn't repair it herself. She asked her neighbour to recommend her a plumber. Mr Grant said she needn't get a plumber and offered to come and mend it himself. Jane told him how grateful she was for his help. Mr Grant thought it ought to be quite easy to mend Jane's tap. He had had to mend one the day before and it had been no problem. Jane wanted to be able to repair a tap herself in future, so she asked Mr Grant to show her what to do. He explained that first she had to take the top off the tap. But he was unable to move the top. Even with a large wrench and a rag he wasn't able to move it. With a tremendous effort he finally moved the nut. Unfortunately this broke the tap and water was everywhere. Mr Grant should have turned the water off first. It was a terrible mess and Jane had to call the plumber.

A friend in need is a friend indeed

Vocabulary			Wortschatz
32	life, pl lives	laɪf, laɪvz	Leben
	friendly	'frendlɪ	freundlich, zuvor-, entgegenkommend
	helpful	'helpfʊl	hilfsbereit
	unfriendly	ʌn'frendlɪ	unfreundlich
	fence	fens	(Garten-)Zaun
	activity	æk'tɪvətɪ	Tätigkeit, Geschäftigkeit
	contact	'kɒntækt	Beziehung, Anschluß, Kontakt
	lonely	'ləʊnlɪ	einsam
32 A	to drip	tə 'drɪp	tropfen
	mad	mæd	verrückt, wahnsinnig
	to drive s.b. mad	tə draɪv 'mæd	jdn. verrückt machen
	I ought to	aɪ 'ɔ:t tʊ	ich sollte (eigentlich)
	rose	rəʊz	Rose
	around	ə'raʊnd	um . . . herum
	to cut down a tree	tə 'kʌt daʊn ə 'tri:	einen Baum fällen
	Could I ask you a favour?	'kʊd aɪ 'ɑ:sk jʊ ə 'feɪvə	Könnte ich Sie um einen Gefallen bitten?
	I can't stand it any longer.	aɪ 'kɑ:nt 'stænd ɪt enɪ 'lɒŋgə	Ich kann es nicht mehr länger ertragen, aushalten.
	able	'eɪbl	fähig, imstande
	wrench	rentʃ	Schraubenschlüssel
	toolbox	'tu:lbɒks	Werkzeugkasten
	heavy	'hevɪ	schwer
	to lift	tə 'lɪft	hochheben
	strong	strɒŋ	stark
	hockey	'hɒkɪ	Hockey
	in future	ɪn 'fju:tʃə	in Zukunft
	rag	ræg	(Putz-)Lumpen
	towel	'taʊəl	Handtuch
	tea-towel	'ti: taʊəl	Küchenhandtuch
	top	tɒp	obere Seite, Deckel, Kappe
	plumber	'plʌmə	Installateur
	bucket	'bʌkɪt	Eimer
	strength	streŋθ	Kraft, Stärke
	rugby	'rʌgbɪ	Rugby
	turn	tɜ:n	Drehung
	to turn off	tə tɜ:n 'ɒf	abdrehen
	to be allowed to	tə bɪ ə'laʊd tʊ	dürfen
32 B	to have a chat with s.b.	tʃæt	mit jdm. plaudern
	to characterise	tə 'kærəktəraɪz	charakterisieren, schildern, beschreiben
32 C	to share	tə 'ʃeə	teilen
32 E	to count	tə 'kaʊnt	zählen

32 F	necessarily	ˈnesəsərəlɪ	unbedingt, notwendig
32 H	extra	ˈekstrə	zusätzlich, extra
	service	ˈsɜːvɪs	Dienst-, Arbeitsleistung
32 J	to hold	tə ˈhəʊld	abhalten
	housewarming party	ˈhaʊswɔːmɪŋ pɑːtɪ	Hauseinweihungsparty
	to manage	tə ˈmænɪdʒ	etwas schaffen, zustande, zuwege bringen
	to dress up	tə dres ˈʌp	sich fein machen
	around	əˈraʊnd	*hier:* gegen, etwa um . . .
	to join	tə ˈdʒɔɪn	sich treffen, sich begegnen, zusammenkommen
32 K	barbecue	ˈbɑːbɪkjuː	Grill(party)
32 L	smashing	ˈsmæʃɪŋ	großartig, gewaltig
	terrific	təˈrɪfɪk	phantastisch
32 M	tremendous	trɪˈmendəs	schrecklich, furchtbar
	effort	ˈefət	Anstrengung
	nut	nʌt	Schraubenmutter
	unfortunately	ʌnˈfɔːtʃnətlɪ	unglücklicherweise, leider
	mess	mes	Unordnung, Durcheinander

32

UNIT 33

A police station

(CB) Visitors to Britain are usually very impressed by the British police. They find them extremely friendly and helpful. Most British people share this good opinion. Children grow up with the idea of the policeman as a friend. The fact that the police don't normally carry guns helps this image.
Scotland Yard is a famous police department. There's hardly any detective story or thriller without an officer from the Yard. This fiction does not give a true picture of reality. Scotland Yard has a department called "Special Branch". This is the secret service and it is their job to catch spies.

33 A At the police station

(J = Jane, R = Russell, F = Fred)

J There's been a burglary.
They've stolen my safe.
They broke into my house.
I saw them get away.
You've got to catch them.
Hurry up!

R Now just calm down, madam.
What are you talking about?
Who broke into your house?
Who got away?

J The burglars, of course.

R Do stop worrying, madam.
Tell me what happened.

J I'd just come home from the party.
I was going to put my jewels in the safe when I heard voices.

R Where did the voices come from?

J They came from the living-room.
And then I saw them.

R Who did you see?

J Who did I see?
The two men of course.
I saw them through the glass door.

R Just a moment, madam.
I have to write all this down.
Where did this happen?
What's your name?
J Mrs James Baker.
R And your address, please, Mrs Baker?
J 22 Belgrave Mews, London WC2.

R I see.
Now, tell me exactly what you saw.
What time did you come home?
J I got back home at about half past eleven.
R Were there any witnesses?
Who saw you?
J There weren't any witnesses, I'm afraid.
Nobody saw me.
R Do go on. What did you see?
J The light was on in the living-room.
R Who had put the light on?
J The burglars had put it on.
They were talking quite loudly and I listened to them.
R What were they talking about?
J About the safe of course.
They wanted to get it open.
They were trying to find out the combination.
R Who does the safe belong to?
J It belongs to my husband and me.
R What's in it?
J All my jewels, a diamond necklace, some very valuable rings and some documents.
We don't believe in banks.
R I don't agree with you there.
Now do go on with the story, please.
Did they manage to get the safe open?
J No, they couldn't find out the combination.
Then they started to argue.
R What did they argue about?
J Well, one of them wanted to take the whole safe away. The other one wanted to blow it open.
R And what was the safe like?
Could you describe it?
J It's about the size of a television set.
It's very heavy.
R Where was the safe?
J It was in a cupboard in the living-room.
R Why didn't you tell me that before?
J But I did tell you.
R No, you didn't.
There's nothing about it here.
J Oh, I'm terribly sorry,
I do apologise.

R Now do go on. What happened next?
J They were still arguing when I heard a whistle.
R A whistle?
Where did it come from?
J It came from the garden.
One of them said: "Okay sir, that's the signal. We've got to be quick.
Let's hurry up."
R What did they do then?
J They pulled the safe out of the cupboard and then they carried it away.

R Where did they take it to?

J They put it into a car and drove off.
Then I came here straight away.

R That was the right thing to do.
I'm very glad you came.
Jack, Fred, come in here a moment, will you?

F Phew, it's heavy.
Let's get rid of this.

J What?
You've caught them already!

R Are these the two burglars?

J Yes, and that's my safe.
Lock them up! They're dangerous!

F Who do you think is dangerous?
Who do you want to lock up?

R Just a minute, Mrs Baker.
Would you please tell us the combination number?
We'd like to look inside the safe.

J Oh, I can't remember the number.
I've forgotten it.

R That doesn't matter. We've already found it out.

J What are you doing?
You aren't allowed to open my safe.
What are you looking for?

(R takes a radio transmitter out of the safe)

R That's what we were looking for.
Very nice "jewellery".
I know why you don't believe in banks.
(to his colleagues)
She must be quite an important spy.

J Spy? What are you talking about?
What do you take me for?
This must be a mistake.
Who put those things in there?

R You did.
I arrest you as a spy.
You are not obliged to say anything unless you wish to do so, but what you say may be put into writing and given in evidence.

33 B Questions

Where did Jane spend her evening?
What time did she come home?
What does the word "witness" mean?
Where was the safe?
Who does the safe belong to?
Why did Jane go to the police station?
What did the police find in the safe?
What happened to Jane at the end of the story?
What do you call a person who steals something?

33 C And you?

Would you like to work at a police station?
Why (not)? Give reasons.
The ideal policeman is one who . . . . Give your definition.

33 D Phrasal verbs — Verben mit Zusatzwörtern

Who had **put** the light **on?**	*Wer hatte das Licht angemacht?*
Do you **get on with** her?	*Kommst du mit ihr aus?*
She doesn't **believe in** banks.	*Sie traut den Banken nicht.*
I saw them **get away.**	*Ich sah sie entkommen.*
They wanted to **get** the safe **open.**	*Sie wollten den Safe öffnen.*
He **turned down** my offer.	*Er lehnte mein Angebot ab.*
Why do you **put up with** it?	*Warum finden Sie sich damit ab?*
Take your coat **off.**	*Legen Sie Ihren Mantel ab.*
They wanted to **get rid of** the box.	*Sie wollten die Kiste loswerden.*
She **rang** him **up.**	*Sie rief ihn an.*
We'll **blow** it **open.**	*Wir werden ihn (= den Safe) in die Luft sprengen.*
Can you **find out** his address?	*Kannst du seine Adresse herausfinden?*
Do **get on with** it!	*Mach endlich weiter!*

Eine Reihe von Verben wird in Verbindung mit Zusatzwörtern verwendet, die eng zum Verb gehören. Man kann die Bedeutung solcher Verbindungen aus Verb + Zusatzwort nicht mehr vom Grundverb ableiten, sondern muß sie wie eine neue Vokabel lernen.
Wir empfehlen Ihnen, eine Kartei mit Beispielsätzen anzulegen und sich diese Beispiele gut einzuprägen, denn in diese Kategorie fallen ziemlich viele der alltäglich verwendeten englischen Verben.

33 E Translate the sentences. Use a phrasal verb:

Ich kann mit meiner Arbeit nicht vorankommen.
Warum läßt du dir solche Arbeitsbedingungen gefallen?
Kannst du ausfindig machen, wer es getan hat?
Gelang es der Polizei, die Tür zu öffnen?
Die Einbrecher hatten das Licht angemacht.
Er konnte das Klavier nicht loswerden.
Ich werde ihn gleich anrufen.
Wir sprachen gerade über ein wichtiges Problem.

33 F Interrogative pronouns — Fragepronomen

a) who

Who saw you?	*Wer sah dich?*
Who broke into your house?	*Wer ist in Ihr Haus eingebrochen?*

"Who" fragt nach Personen. Fragen nach dem Subjekt stehen in der normalen Reihenfolge:
Who (Subjekt) – saw (Verb) – you (Objekt)?

Who do you want to see?	*Wen möchten Sie sehen?*
Who did you see?	*Wen sahst du?*
Who does the safe belong to?	*Wem gehört der Safe?*
Who did you travel with?	*Mit wem sind Sie gereist?*

Bei Fragen nach dem Objekt haben wir die Fragestellung mit "do", "does" oder "did" nach dem Fragewort.
In der Schriftsprache finden Sie die Objektform "whom", z. B.: Whom did you see?
Präpositionen stehen in diesen Fragesätzen am Satzende.

b) whose

Whose mother complained about the noise?	*Wessen Mutter beklagte sich über den Lärm?*
Whose safe did they take away?	*Wessen Safe haben sie weggenommen?*

Das Fragepronomen "whose" kann bei einem Subjekt oder einem Objekt stehen.

c) what / which

What were they talking about?	*Worüber haben sie gesprochen?*
What do you take me for?	*Wofür halten Sie mich?*
What are you waiting for?	*Worauf warten Sie?*
Which film did you like better, "Love Story" or "Casablanca"?	*Welcher Film gefiel dir besser, „Love Story" oder „Casablanca"?*
Which of you brought the money?	*Wer von euch brachte das Geld?*

"What" fragt nach Sachen, nach Eigenschaften und Erläuterungen ganz allgemein.
"Which" fragt nach Personen und Sachen und zwar immer aus einer begrenzten Anzahl.

33 G Fill in the missing interrogative pronoun:

. . . . . were you smiling at?
. . . . . European language is the easiest to learn?
. . . . . colour is your car?
. . . . . time did you leave?
. . . . . do you want to lock up?
. . . . . letter is more important, the one to New York or the one to Washington?
. . . . . got away?
. . . . . is this safe?
. . . . . can I show you?
. . . . . helped you with your work?
. . . . . do you know about the robbery?

33 H Ask questions: ⚇

Jane went out last night. *Fragen Sie, mit wem sie ausgegangen ist.*
The books belong to Russell. *Fragen Sie, welche Bücher Russell gehören.*
He gave her the key. *Fragen Sie, wessen Schlüssel er ihr gegeben hat.*
Fred spoke to a girl. *Fragen Sie, mit wem er gesprochen hat.*
The police caught two thieves. *Fragen Sie, wer die Diebe waren.*
Jane wants to see somebody. *Fragen Sie, wen sie sehen möchte.*
Your friends were talking about politics. *Fragen Sie, worüber sie sich unterhalten haben.*
The light was on in the living-room. *Fragen Sie, wer das Licht angemacht hat.*

33 I Emphatic "do" — Verstärkender Gebrauch von "do"

I **do** apologise.	*Es tut mir wirklich sehr leid.*
I **do** understand your difficulties.	*Ich verstehe Ihre Schwierigkeiten wirklich.*
I **did** tell you.	*Ich habe es Ihnen doch gesagt.*
Do sit down.	*Setzen Sie sich doch.*
Do go on with the story, please.	*Fahren Sie doch bitte mit der Geschichte fort.*

Ein vor dem Hauptverb stehendes "do" ist stark betont und verleiht der Aussage besonderen Nachdruck.
Auch der bejahte Imperativ kann mit "do" verstärkt werden.
Im Deutschen verwenden wir hierfür meist Wörter wie *doch, ja, bloß, wirklich, bitte.*

33

33 J A report

You were the witness of a car accident. Give a report about the following points: where and when the accident happened, where you were and what you were doing, whose fault it was, whether there were other witnesses.

33 K Give the German equivalents:

Die englische Sprache bildet zahlreiche Wortzusammensetzungen. Wie lautet die deutsche Entsprechung zu folgenden Beispielen?

eyewitness – teabag – swimsuit – shopping list – value added tax – revolving door – number plate – typing mistake – bath towel – spy ring – drinking water – theatre-goer – election forecast – police car

33 L Put in the correct noun of the word given in brackets: ⚇

What (invent) are you talking about?	You must get medical (treat).
There was an important (discover).	Wouldn't you like to make a little (speak)?
They were engaged in a long (argue).	I wasn't impressed by his (strong).
He works in the (develop) department.	We got an (invite) to a dinner-party.

33 M Situation – Say it in English

Fragen Sie jemanden, ob er zufällig weiß, wo hier ein Telefon ist.
Bitten Sie jemanden, Ihnen zu sagen, wo die nächste Polizeistation ist.
Sagen Sie, daß auf der M4 ein Unfall passiert ist.
Sagen Sie, daß jemand in ein anderes Auto gefahren ist.
Sagen Sie Ihrem Gesprächspartner, daß Sie Zeuge sein werden, wenn er einen braucht.
Ihr Gesprächspartner bedankt sich für die Hilfsbereitschaft.
Sie werden gefragt, wie das andere Auto ausgesehen hat.
Man fordert Sie auf, genau zu schildern, was Sie gesehen haben.

33 N Summary

Jane went to the police station to report a burglary at her house. She was very worried. The policeman on duty asked her to tell him exactly what had happened. Jane told him that she had been to a party and was just going to put her jewels away in the safe when she heard voices in the living-room. They were talking about how to open the safe. It seems they couldn't work out the combination. One burglar wanted to blow it open and the other wanted to take away the whole safe.
Jane said she saw them put the safe in a car and drive off. The policeman then asked her what was in the safe. According to Jane it contained all her valuable jewellery, rings, and a necklace, as well as some documents.
The sergeant called to a couple of men in another room. They came in – very slowly because they were carrying Jane's safe. Jane cried out and told the sergeant to lock the two burglars up immediately – she recognised the men she had seen in her flat. But the sergeant only smiled and told the two policemen to open the safe. It didn't contain jewellery. It contained everything an important spy needs. The "burglars" had been looking for the evidence they needed to arrest Jane as a spy.

Watch out!

Vocabulary			Wortschatz
33	to impress	tʊ ɪm'pres	beeindrucken
	police	pə'li:s	Polizei
	to grow up	tə grəʊ 'ʌp	aufwachsen
	fact	fækt	Tatsache
	gun	gʌn	Gewehr
	image	'ɪmɪdʒ	Vorstellung, Bild
	hardly	'hɑ:dlɪ	kaum
	thriller	'θrɪlə	Sensationsfilm
	without	wɪ'ðaʊt	ohne
	officer	'ɒfɪsə	(Polizei-)Beamter
	fiction	'fɪkʃn	Vorstellung, freie Erfindung
	reality	rɪ'ælətɪ	Wirklichkeit
	branch	brɑ:ntʃ	Abteilung
	secret service	'si:krət 's3:vɪs	Geheimdienst
	spy	spaɪ	Spion(in)
33 A	police station	pə'li:s steɪʃn	Polizeirevier
	burglary	'b3:glərɪ	(Einbruchs-)Diebstahl
	to steal, stole, stolen	tə 'sti:l, 'stəʊl, stəʊlən	stehlen
	safe	seɪf	Safe
	to get away	tə get ə'weɪ	fortschaffen, wegbringen, entkommen
	to calm down	tə kɑ:m 'daʊn	sich beruhigen
	to talk about	tə tɔ:k ə'baʊt	sprechen über
	to break into	tə breɪk 'ɪntʊ	einbrechen
	jewels	'dʒʊəlz	Juwelen, Edelsteine, Schmuck
	glass door	'glɑ:s 'dɔ:	Glastüre
	to write down	tə raɪt 'daʊn	aufschreiben, niederschreiben
	to get back	tə get 'bæk	zurückkommen
	witness	'wɪtnəs	Zeuge, Zeugin
	to put on	tə pʊt 'ɒn	einschalten, anmachen
	to get open	tə get 'əʊpən	öffnen
	combination	kɒmbɪ'neɪʃn	*hier:* Zahlenkombination
	diamond necklace	'daɪəmənd 'nekləs	Diamantenhalsband
	valuable	'væljʊəbl	wertvoll
	ring	rɪŋ	Ring
	documents	'dɒkjʊmənts	Dokumente, Unterlagen
	to argue about	tʊ 'ɑ:gju: ə'baʊt	streiten über, sich unterhalten über
	to blow open	tə bləʊ 'əʊpən	aufsprengen
	cupboard	'kʌbəd	Schrank
	whistle	'wɪsl	Pfiff, Pfeife
	signal	'sɪgnəl	Signal, Zeichen
	to pull out	tə pʊl 'aʊt	herausnehmen, herausreißen
	to drive off	tə draɪv 'ɒf	wegfahren

	straight away	ˈstreɪt əˈweɪ	direkt, gerade, sofort, auf der Stelle
	to get rid of s.th.	tə get ˈrɪd əv	etwas loswerden
	to lock up	tə lɒk ˈʌp	einsperren
	dangerous	ˈdeɪndʒərəs	gefährlich
	to find out	tə faɪnd ˈaʊt	herausfinden
	radio transmitter	ˈreɪdɪəʊ trænsmɪtə	Radiosender
	jewellery	ˈdʒʊəlrɪ	Schmucksachen
	What do you take me for?	teɪk ˈfɔː	Wofür halten Sie mich?
	to arrest s.b.	tʊ əˈrest	jdn. verhaften
	to be obliged to	tə bɪ əˈblaɪdʒd tʊ	verpflichtet sein
	evidence	ˈevɪdəns	Beweis, Beweisstücke
33 B	robber	ˈrɒbə	Räuber
33 C	definition	defɪˈnɪʃn	Erklärung, Definition
33 D	to get on with s.b.	tə get ˈɒn wɪð	mit jdm. auskommen
	to turn down	tə tɜːn ˈdaʊn	ablehnen
33 E	working conditions	ˈwɜːkɪŋ kəndɪʃnz	Arbeitsbedingungen
33 J	point	pɔɪnt	Punkt, Stelle
33 K	eyewitness	ˈaɪwɪtnəs	Augenzeuge, -zeugin
	teabag	ˈtiːbæg	Teebeutel
	swimsuit	ˈswɪmsuːt	Badeanzug
	value added tax	ˈvæljʊ ˈædɪd tæks	Mehrwertsteuer
	revolving door	rɪˈvɒlvɪŋ ˈdɔː	Drehtüre
	number plate	ˈnʌmbə pleɪt	Nummernschild
	theatre-goer	ˈθɪətə gəʊə	Theaterbesucher
	forecast	ˈfɔːkɑːst	Vorhersage
33 L	engaged in s.th.	ɪŋˈgeɪdʒd ɪn	an etwas arbeiten, mit etwas beschäftigt sein
	argument	ˈɑːgjʊmənt	Erörterung, Debatte
33 M	possibly	ˈpɒsəblɪ	möglicherweise, eventuell
33 N	according to	əˈkɔːdɪŋ tʊ	gemäß, nach, laut
	to contain	tə kənˈteɪn	enthalten
	sergeant	ˈsɑːdʒnt	Wachtmeister; Feldwebel
	to cry out	tə kraɪ ˈaʊt	aufschreien
	immediately	ɪˈmiːdjətlɪ	sofort, unmittelbar
	to recognise	tə ˈrekəgnaɪz	(wieder)erkennen

UNIT 34

Burlington Arcade, London

34

CB London is famous for its shops. It's one of the world's great shopping centres. Places like Regent Street, Bond Street, Oxford Street, Piccadilly, Burlington Arcade, Knightsbridge or Kensington High Street offer a wide choice. People who live in London have all kinds of shops on their front doorstep, only a short distance away. But those who live in the country, far away from a big town, often have no other choice than to do their shopping by mail order. Mail order shopping originated in the United States, and is now a multi-million-pound business in Britain.

34 A Mail order shopping ○○

(J = Jane, R = Russell, D = Delivery man)

R Why can't I wear these clothes to Susan's wedding?

J You must be joking!

R Why? This is the suit I wore to Jack's wedding.

J That was ten years ago.
And those clothes don't fit you any more. I haven't got any clothes that I could wear. Why don't we order something new?

R Order? Where from?

J From this mail order firm.

R Mail order firm?
Why don't we just go to Bensons?
Think of all the postage we'll save.

J But the clothes in here are much cheaper than in a shop.
They buy everything in large quantities and don't have to pay any shop assistants.

J Come and have a look at these prices.
R All right.
What have they got?
J Everything.
You can get anything you want by mail order, from cameras to clothes to camping equipment. We can order all the clothes we need.
R Right – I haven't got a single jacket that fits me and I haven't got a dark suit that I can wear to the office.
I think I'm the only one in our office who hasn't got a decent suit.
J And don't forget you need a suit that you can wear to the wedding.
Look – there are some suits here that come with two pairs of trousers.
How about this one?
R Hm – not bad. Quite good in fact.
Quite cheap too.
J That's what I keep telling you.
They're good quality, too.
R At least according to their advertisements.
J Yes, it says here "The best suits money can buy".

R What are we waiting for?
J Just a minute. I need something to write with.
Ah, here's my pen.
I'll fill in the order form.
R Where are the suits which come with two pairs of trousers?
I'd like the dark grey one – that's number HEW 4260.
J HEW 4260.
What size do you take?
R I take size 38 now.
J All right, 38.
Is there anything else you need?
A tie or a shirt?
R Yes, I need a new shirt that goes with the suit.

J Here are the shirts.
Size $15\frac{1}{2}$.
And here's a tie that would go very well with that suit. Let's order that too.
R Right. That's number GAZ 3044.
J GAZ 3044.
R What about you?
J I've already found something I'd like.
There's a very nice dress here.
R Which one are you talking about?
This yellow one?
J No, not the yellow one, the red one.
R That would suit you very well.
What size do you take?
J Size 34.
R That's number PQR 8753.
J PQR 8753.
And I do need a coat which matches it.
We don't want to be the only people at the wedding who look old-fashioned.
The Joneses will be very smart.
R Well, it's their daughter who's getting married, after all.
J Here's a coat that looks nice.
R Yes, that'll be perfect.
It's number YMR 2197.
J YMR 2197.
R What are you looking for?
J I'm looking for a stamp and an envelope. I'll send it off straight away.
How much does it come to?
R £248 plus postage.

(Two weeks later)

J Would you like another cup of tea?

R Yes please.

J Here you are.

(doorbell)

R Who's that?

J I'll go and see who it is.

D Good morning. I've got a parcel for you. Cash on delivery, or you can pay later.

J Where is it from?

D It's from Jackson's – the mail order firm. There's £251.50 to pay.

J I see. I'll pay now.
You will take a cheque, won't you?

D Yes, if you've got a cheque card.

J Here you are – £251.50, and here's my cheque card.

D Sign here, please.

R Who were you talking to?

J The delivery man from Jackson's.
The clothes we ordered have come.

R Oh, good!
Now let's see what they've sent us.

J Ah, this is the suit you ordered.
Hm – it looks a bit smaller than the ones you normally wear.

R Jane! It's much too small!
I can't possibly wear this!
What on earth were they thinking of?
They must have sent the wrong size.

J Ah, and here's the red dress I ordered.
It's tiny! This isn't my size!

R So much for your mail order shopping.
I'll write a letter of complaint immediately and we must stop that cheque at once.
(R begins to type)
Dear Sirs,
I wish to make a complaint about the order we placed on August 16.
All the clothes you sent us are the wrong size.

J Hey – look here.
I think we're the ones who made the mistake. "All sizes in this catalogue are continental. For British sizes see the table below."

J/R Everything we ordered is too small!

34 B Questions

Why do Jane and Russell order their clothes from a mail order firm?
When do they want to wear the clothes for the first time?
When did they place the order?
What did Russell order?
What did Jane order?
How did they pay for the parcel?
How much did they pay?
Did they get the right clothes?

34 C And you?

Have you ever done your shopping by mail order?
Give reasons why (or why not).

34 D Relative pronouns (I)

persons	things
who **(that)**	**which** **that**

a) Relativpronomen als Subjekt des Verbs

I'm the only one **who** hasn't got a decent suit.

We're the only people **who** look old-fashioned.

Where are the suits | **that** / **which** | come with two pairs of trousers?

I need a coat | **that** / **which** | matches the dress.

The suit | **that** / **which** | doesn't fit.

The girl | **who** / **that** | lives next door.

Die Form des Relativpronomens ist für Singular und Plural gleich.
"Who" steht für Personen.
"Which" steht für Sachen.
"That" kann für Sachen und gelegentlich auch für Personen stehen.

b) Relativpronomen als Objekt des Verbs

He is the most interesting person **(who)** / **(that)** I ever met.

The book **(which)** / **(that)** I read last night was a thriller.

Ist das Relativpronomen Objekt, wird es im gesprochenen Englisch meist weggelassen. Haupt- und Relativsatz stehen dann unverbunden nebeneinander.

34 E Fill in "who", "which" or "that" where necessary: ○○

I haven't got a coat . . . . . . matches my new dress.
The car . . . . . . he is driving is not his.
He doesn't know the man . . . . . . lives next door.
The house . . . . . . we saw in Canterbury is for sale.
The parcel . . . . . . came this morning was for Jane and Russell.
Jane likes the girl . . . . works in her office.

A lot of tourists . . . . . . come to London every year want to see the Changing of the Guard.
The car . . . . . . he was driving overturned.
Are you sure this is the book . . . . . . you want?
You can't get alcoholic drinks in restaurants . . . . . . are not fully licensed.

34 F Prepositions in relative clauses — Präpositionen in Relativsätzen

The man I was speaking **to.**	*Der Mann, mit dem ich gesprochen habe.*
The clothes we were talking **about.**	*Die Kleider, über die wir gesprochen haben.*

Im gesprochenen Englisch stehen Präpositionen meist am Ende des Relativsatzes. Im Deutschen stehen sie dagegen vor dem Relativpronomen.

34 G Translate the sentences:

Der Katalog, den ich gerade angeschaut habe.
Die Briefmarken, die Humphrey gerade gesucht hat.
Der Mann, dem ich das Auto verkaufte.
Die Leute, mit denen ich arbeite.
Die Musik, die du gerade anhörst.
Die Eintrittskarten, nach denen Sie fragten.
Das Thema, über das wir diskutierten.
Der Artikel, mit dem Sie nicht einverstanden waren.

34 H A letter of complaint

5 September 19..

The Big Stores
29 Blackheath
Morden Mews
London SE3 OAE

Dear Sir or Madam,

I am writing to make a complaint about a skirt I bought for £25 at your store a week ago. Two days later I got very wet in heavy rain and by the time I got home the skirt was well above my knees and looked like a mini-skirt.
As the manufacturer's label describes it as fully shrink-proof, I would be grateful if you would either exchange the skirt for a similar one or refund my £25.

I look forward to hearing from you.

Yours faithfully,

Jane Egan

34 I Write a letter of complaint

You've ordered some electrical equipment by mail order (e. g. a coffee-machine, an electric tin-opener, a toaster, a shaver, an electric toothbrush etc.) that doesn't work. Give reasons for your complaint.

34 J Some useful expressions for shopping

Shop assistant: Good afternoon. Can I help you?
Customer: I'm looking for a shirt (dress).
Shop assistant: What size do you take?
Customer: My German size is 38.
Shop assistant: What colour were you thinking of?
Customer: Pink or blue, perhaps.
Shop assistant: Let's see what we've got.
How about this one?
Customer: It looks nice. Can I try it on, please?
How much is it?
Shop assistant: It's £35.
Customer: That's more than I wanted to spend.
Have you got something more reasonable?
Shop assistant: Would you like to try this one on?
Customer: No, I'm afraid it's not quite what I was looking for.
Thank you. Goodbye.

Sizes

W.-Germany	36 38 40 42 44 46 48
Great Britain	32 34 36 38 40 42 44

34 K To wear – to carry – to bear

Welche dieser Entsprechungen für das deutsche Wort „tragen" paßt in den folgenden Sätzen?

He never .... an umbrella.
Russell is .... a bow tie.
I can't .... this nonsense.
It's cold. Why aren't you .... a coat?
British policemen don't usually .... guns.

34 L Situation – Say it in English

Sagen Sie, daß Sie einen warmen Mantel suchen.
Der Verkäufer möchte wissen, welche Größe Sie haben.
Sagen Sie, daß Sie Größe 40 tragen.
Fragen Sie, ob er diesen Mantel auch in anderen Farben hat.
Der Verkäufer sagt, daß Ihnen der blaue Mantel besonders gut steht.
Sagen Sie, daß Sie diesen Mantel nehmen werden.
Sagen Sie, daß Sie ein Halstuch möchten, das zu Ihrem Mantel paßt.
Fragen Sie, ob Sie mit Euroscheck bezahlen können.

34 M Summary

Jane and Russell had received an invitation to a wedding. They decided to order some new clothes from a mail order firm, as Jane said they would then be cheaper than in an ordinary shop. Russell needed a new suit for the office which would also be right for the wedding. He ordered a dark grey suit and a shirt and tie to match. Naturally, Jane also wanted some clothes for the wedding, so she ordered a red dress that she liked in the catalogue, as well as a coat that she found very smart. When they had chosen all the clothes, they sent the order off immediately.

Two weeks later the parcel with the clothes arrived and they couldn't wait to open it. They both got a nasty shock when they saw the clothes. Everything they had ordered was much too small. There was nothing they could possibly wear to the wedding. Russell was so angry that he fetched his typewriter and started to write a letter of complaint to the firm. Jane checked the details in the catalogue again and they both had another surprise – they had overlooked the fact that the sizes in the catalogue were continental sizes.

Small is beautiful

Vocabulary			Wortschatz
34	distance	'dɪstəns	Entfernung
	mail order	'meɪl ɔ:də	Bestellung durch die Post
	to originate	tʊ ə'rɪdʒəneɪt	herkommen, herstammen
	multi-million-pound business	'mʌltɪ mɪljən paʊnd 'bɪznɪs	Multimillionen-Pfund-Geschäft
34 A	delivery man	dɪ'lɪvərɪ mæn	Lieferbote
	postage	'pəʊstɪdʒ	Postgebühren
	quantity	'kwɒntətɪ	Menge
	camping equipment	'kæmpɪŋ ɪkwɪpmənt	Camping-Ausrüstung
	decent	'di:sənt	anständig, ordentlich
	a pair of trousers	ə 'peər əv 'traʊzəz	eine Hose
	I keep telling you	aɪ 'ki:p 'telɪŋ jʊ	ich sage dir doch dauernd
	advertisement	əd'vɜ:tɪsmənt	Reklame, Werbung; Anzeige
	order form	'ɔ:də fɔ:m	Bestellschein
	tie	taɪ	Krawatte
	to go with	tə gəʊ 'wɪð	passen zu
	to suit	tə 'su:t	passen
	to match	tə 'mætʃ	(zusammen)passen
	smart	smɑ:t	elegant, schick, fein
	daughter	'dɔ:tə	Tochter

	envelope	ˈenvələʊp, ˈɒnvələʊp	Umschlag, Briefkuvert
	cash on delivery	ˈkæʃ ɒn dɪˈlɪvərɪ	Bezahlung bei Lieferung
	cheque	tʃek	Scheck
	cheque card	ˈtʃek kɑːd	Scheckkarte
	tiny	taɪnɪ	winzig
	complaint	kəmˈpleɪnt	Beschwerde
	to place an order	tə ˈpleɪs ən ˈɔːdə	einen Auftrag erteilen
	hey!	heɪ	he! heda!
	table	ˈteɪbl	(Übersichts-)Tafel, Tabelle
34 E	sale	seɪl	Verkauf
	to overturn	tʊ əʊvəˈtɜːn	überschlagen
34 H	knee	niː	Knie
	manufacturer	mænjʊˈfæktʃərə	Fabrikant, Hersteller
	label	ˈleɪbl	Etikett
	shrink-proof	ˈʃrɪŋkpruːf	nicht einlaufend
	to exchange	tʊ ɪksˈtʃeɪndʒ	umtauschen
	similar	ˈsɪmɪlə	ähnlich
	to refund	tə riːˈfʌnd	(Geld) zurückerstatten
	to look forward to	tə lʊk ˈfɔːwəd tʊ	entgegensehen, erwarten
34 I	electrical	ɪˈlektrɪkl	elektrisch
	equipment	ɪˈkwɪpmənt	Ausrüstung, Ausstattung
	toaster	ˈtəʊstə	Toastapparat
	toothbrush	ˈtuːθbrʌʃ	Zahnbürste
34 J	expression	ɪkˈspreʃn	Ausdruck
	pink	pɪŋk	rosafarben, rötlich
	to try on	tə traɪ ˈɒn	anprobieren
34 K	to bear	tə ˈbeə	(er)tragen
34 L	blue	bluː	blau
34 M	to overlook	tʊ əʊvəˈlʊk	übersehen, mißachten

UNIT 35

A bridge over the River Liffey in Dublin

CB

The Republic of Ireland is an independent country. It has two Houses of Parliament, an elected President who is Head of State and a Taoiseach (Prime Minister) who is Head of Government. The capital city is Dublin.

35

Ireland is particularly rich in ancient monuments. Relics from the Stone Age show that Ireland has been inhabited for about 8,000 years. Tribes from central Europe reached the island in the pre-Christian era. The language they spoke was Celtic. St. Patrick, the Irish national saint, brought Christianity to the Irish people.

One of St. Patrick's innovations was the system of monasteries, around which all church activities centred. The monks illustrated famous manuscripts such as the Book of Kells, which is on display at Trinity College, Dublin. During the 10th century Vikings settled in many parts of the country. The "round towers" are the most typical buildings of that time.

In the 12th century King Henry III of England arrived on the scene. England was a Norman kingdom at that time. The Anglo-Norman occupation brought profound changes to Ireland. The occupants introduced the feudal system of government. All land belonged to the king who granted it to others in return for their services. England ruled most of Ireland. King Henry VIII was the first king who called himself "King of Ireland". He tried to introduce the Reformation into Ireland, but the majority of the people remained Catholic.

One of the worst disasters of 19th century Europe was the great Irish potato famine. Over a million died of starvation, another million emigrated to America and about half that number to Britain. This intensified the anti-Irish reaction of the British.

In the Easter Rising of 1916 the Irish proclaimed a provisional government for the Irish Republic. The war ended in December 1921 with the partition of Ireland, but six counties in the north where the majority of the population are Protestant remained part of the United Kingdom.

35 A A tour of Ireland

(J = Jane, R = Russell, A = American, B = Barkeeper)

B Now, where's the couple who ordered two Irish coffees?
R Here we are.
B Here's the coffee you ordered. That'll be £2.80.
R Here you are. Keep the change.
J Ah, this is just what I needed. Cheers, Russell!
R Cheers, Jane!
A Excuse me, is that seat taken?
R No, it isn't. It's free.
A Thank you. Can I ask you a question?
R Yes, go ahead.
A What's that you're drinking?
J It's Irish coffee.
A Is it different from ordinary coffee?
R Yes, indeed. It's got Irish whiskey in it –
J and a spoonful of cream on the top.
A That sounds good. Just the drink I need.

A Barkeeper!
B What can I do for you, sir?
A I'd like an Irish coffee too.
B Certainly, sir.
A Have you been here long?
J Well, we've been in Dublin for a week now.
A I only arrived here today.
R Where did you come from?
A I came from Holyhead to Dun . . . I've forgotten how they pronounce the name of that place.
J Dun Laoghaire.
A Yes, that's right, Dun Laoghaire. Now that I've finished the business I went to Britain for I can take the holiday I need.
R You should see something of Ireland while you're here. How much time have you got?
A I've got all the time I need. I've got a whole week. But I don't know Ireland. I've no idea what the most important sights are and where to find them.
J Ireland is a country you need a lot of time for. A week is a bit short.
A Do you think so? I want to see all the sights in Dublin and then I'm going to visit my cousin, who lives in Limerick.
J I wonder why so many Americans have got relatives in Ireland.
A Well, a lot of people emigrated from Ireland after the great potato famine in 1846. My great-great-grandfather, who left Ireland in 1850, left two brothers and a sister here. Their children are distant cousins of mine. Do you have relatives here too?
J Yes. My elder sister, who married an Irishman, has been living here for eight years.

R What do you want to see in Dublin?
A Well, what do you suggest? I want to see everything you can see in one day.
R What! Everything in one day? This is what our relatives gave us. Ireland – where to go, what to do. It tells you what to visit and how to get there.
J My sister, whose husband works at the Irish Tourist Office, gave me these brochures. You can have them if you like.
A That's extremely kind of you!
J Not at all. We've got plenty more.

A Is this in Dublin?

R Yes, that's Trinity College. You shouldn't miss the Book of Kells, which is in the Library there. It's one of the most beautiful old manuscripts in the world.

A And where is this?

R I'm not sure where that is.

J That's Glendalough – it's a ruined monastery about 30 miles south of Dublin.

Glendalough

A Can you tell me how to get there?

R There's a map in this brochure. You'll need a car to get there. Have you got one?

A No, not yet. I'll have to rent one. Do you know what this tower is?

J It's a round tower. It says here: "The monks built the round towers as protection for themselves and their riches against the Vikings, whose main interest was stealing gold and silver."

A Is that a guide book you're reading from?

J No, it's one of the brochures I got from my sister.

R Another interesting day-trip from Dublin would be to Mellifont Abbey, which was one of the first monasteries in Ireland.

Cashel

A Well, that sure sounds interesting . . . All those ruins . . .

J Perhaps you'd be more interested in Newgrange, whose prehistoric burial grounds are really worth a visit.

A Oh, that looks good.

J When will you be leaving Dublin?

A My cousin is expecting me the day after tomorrow in Limerick.

R Well, you can start with Glendalough and before you go to Limerick you must visit Cashel, which was the seat of the Kings of Munster.

J And on your way back to Dublin you should follow the River Shannon to Clonmacnois. It's got a beautiful Celtic cross.

A I've written all that down. Thank you very much. I must be off now.

R Enjoy your trip.

A Thank you. And thanks for all your help. Goodbye.

(Four days later J and R are visiting Clonmacnois.)

J Here we are. The Cross of the Scriptures.

A Hi there! What a surprise!

R Hello! Fancy meeting you here.

J Hello!

Clonmacnois

A You guys certainly gave me plenty to look at! And I've seen everything you suggested – Glendalough, Cashel and now Clonmacnois.

R You've seen all that, and you visited your relatives too, in four days?

A Yes, I've seen everything, so I'm flying home two days earlier. It was a marvellous holiday. Bye!

R He did Ireland in four days. That must be a record.

35 B Questions

What's the capital of the Irish Republic?
What country is Northern Ireland a part of?
What's the name of the patron saint of Ireland?
Why did so many Irish people emigrate to America during the last century?
Who is the Head of Government in the Republic of Ireland?
Where can you see the Book of Kells?
When was the Easter Rising?

35 C And you?

Where are you planning to spend your holiday next summer?
Write a letter to the Tourist Board of the place you want to go and ask for information, for an accommodation guide and for tips on touring around.

35 D Relative pronouns (II) — Relativpronomen

persons	things
whose	**whose (of which)**

This is the man **whose** wife works for us.
It was a meeting **whose** purpose was unclear.

"Whose" ist das Relativpronomen für den Besitzfall. Es steht für Personen und Sachen. In der Schriftsprache finden Sie bei Sachen auch gelegentlich "of which" für "whose", z. B.: It was a meeting the purpose of which was unclear.

35 E Relative clauses — Relativsätze

a) Defining relative clauses — Notwendige Relativsätze

Is that the woman who works at the Irish Tourist Office?
He's a man (that) people like at first sight.

Diese Beispielsätze hätten ohne nähere Bestimmung, d. h. ohne Relativsätze keinen Sinn. Der Relativsatz ist hier für das Verständnis des Hauptsatzes notwendig, er steht in ganz enger Beziehung zu der Bedeutung des Hauptsatzes und darf deshalb nicht durch ein Komma vom Hauptsatz getrennt werden.

b) Non-defining relative clauses — Entbehrliche Relativsätze

My elder sister, **who married an Irishman,** has been living here for eight years.
My sister, **who(m) you met at the party,** lives in Dublin.
My sister, **whose husband works at the Irish Tourist Board,** gave me these brochures.
The Cliffs of Moher, **which rise nearly 700 feet above the Atlantic,** are really worth a visit.

Diese Relativsätze liefern eine zusätzliche Information, die für das Verständnis des Hauptsatzes nicht notwendig, nicht entscheidend ist. Die Bedeutung des Hauptsatzes wird auch ohne den Relativsatz klar. Diese nicht notwendigen, entbehrlichen Relativsätze werden zwischen Kommas gesetzt; sie kommen häufig in der Schriftsprache vor. Sie werden bei Personen mit "who", im Besitzfall mit "whose", in der Schriftsprache im Objektfall auch mit "whom", bei Sachen mit "which" eingeleitet, jedoch niemals mit "that". Im Objektfall darf das Relativpronomen bei entbehrlichen Relativsätzen nicht wegfallen.

35 F Put in the relative pronoun and the commas where necessary:

People . . . . . come to Ireland usually want to see Clonmacnois.
Ireland . . . . . is a member of the Common Market is an independent country.
Trinity College . . . . . houses the Book of Kells is Dublin's University.
Are you the gentleman . . . . . car is parked on the double yellow lines?
The man . . . . . they met in the pub was an American.
Where's the book . . . . . I gave you?
St. Patrick . . . . . lived in the 5th century is Ireland's patron saint.
Dublin . . . . . lies on the River Liffey is the capital of Ireland.
He's a man . . . . . words you can believe.
The General Post Office . . . . . was the scene of the Easter Rising of 1916 is a historic monument.

35 G Dependent (indirect) questions — Abhängige (indirekte) Fragesätze

direkte Frage:	When does the museum open?
indirekte Frage:	I've no idea when the museum opens.
direkte Frage:	Who ordered two coffees?
indirekte Frage:	Do you know who ordered two coffees?
direkte Frage:	What should I do?
indirekte Frage:	I don't know what to do.

a) Bei indirekten Fragen gilt die normale Wortstellung: Subjekt-Verb-Objekt. Die Umschreibung mit "do" bzw. "does" fällt weg.

b) Verwechseln Sie indirekte Fragesätze nicht mit Relativsätzen: Do you know who ordered two coffees? (indirekter Fragesatz); Do you know the gentleman who ordered two coffees? (Relativsatz)

c) Beinhalten die abhängigen Fragesätze eine Anweisung, einen Rat, eine Empfehlung, dann können wir den Satz verkürzen, es genügt der Infinitiv mit "to": Anstelle von "I've no idea what I should do" können wir sagen "I've no idea what to do".

35 H I've no idea . . .

Stellen Sie indirekte Fragen. Beginnen Sie Ihren Satz mit "I've no idea", "I don't know" oder "Could you tell me". Verkürzen Sie, wo dies möglich ist.

Where shall we go?
Who should I invite?
When is his birthday?
What shall I do?
Why does he work on Sunday?
What should we see in Dublin?
When does the plane take off?
What should I suggest?
How can I get there?
When shall we go to Ireland?

35 I Irish money (CB)

Ireland has got its own currency, the Irish pound or punt. There are a hundred pence in a pound.

Notes are issued in 1, 5, 10, 20, 50 and 100 pound notes.
Coins come in ½, 1, 2, 5, 10 and 50 p pieces.

35 J Language (CB)

English is the main language in Ireland although Irish Gaelic is the first official language according to the Constitution. Irish Gaelic is a Celtic language related to Scottish Gaelic and Welsh.

35 K Irish Authors (CB)

Ireland's contribution to world literature is enormous. Many Irish authors wrote in English. Here are the names of some Irish writers and story-tellers.

JONATHAN SWIFT (1667–1745), author of *Gulliver's Travels.* He defended the rights of the poor. Writing, however, was only a part-time job. Swift was also the Dean of St. Patrick's Cathedral in Dublin.

OSCAR WILDE (1854–1900), famous wit, playwright and poet. Some of his most famous plays are *The Picture of Dorian Gray, The Importance of Being Earnest.*

GEORGE BERNARD SHAW (1856–1950) was born in Dublin, but he spent most of his life in England. He wrote plays like *Pygmalion, Arms and the Man, Man and Superman.* In 1925 he won the Nobel Prize for literature.

WILLIAM BUTLER YEATS (1865–1939), also won the Nobel Prize for literature. His poems sang of the Irish land, its legends and heroes.

JAMES JOYCE (1882–1941), a modern novelist. He wrote *Dubliners, Finnegans Wake,* and *Ulysses.*

tion – Say it in English

ußen Sie einen Gast sehr freundlich.
agen Sie, daß Sie sich freuen, daß er kommen konnte.
Einer der Gäste glaubt, einen Bekannten wiederzuerkennen.
Ein Gast ist überrascht, Sie auf der Party anzutreffen.
Wie drückt er diese Überraschung aus?
Fordern Sie Ihre Gäste auf, sich mit Getränken zu bedienen.
Einer der Gäste sagt, daß er jetzt gehen muß.
Sagen Sie, daß es schade ist, daß er nicht länger bleiben kann.
Sagen Sie, daß er bald wieder kommen muß.
Sagen Sie, daß er Ihnen immer willkommen ist.
Ihr Gast bedankt sich für den schönen Abend.
Fragen Sie einen Gast, ob Sie ihn ein Stück mitnehmen können.
Der Angesprochene ist sehr froh über dieses Angebot. Wie reagiert er?
Und wie reagieren Sie darauf?

35 M Summary

This year Jane and Russell went to Ireland for their summer holidays. Neither of them had been there before and they looked forward to three interesting and relaxing weeks. In Dublin they met an American tourist who was having a drink in the same bar. The American spoke to them. He asked what it was that they were drinking, and, when he found out that Irish coffee had whiskey in it and cream on top, he ordered one for himself. He was a friendly and rather talkative man who was touring Ireland by himself. He'd been in Britain on business and had decided to take a short holiday. He wasn't very certain about the sights he should see, so he asked Jane and Russell for advice. As Jane's brother-in-law, who worked for the Irish Tourist Board, had given them a lot of information, they were able to help the American. His problem was that he had only six days to see everything!

A few days later Jane and Russell were visiting the famous Celtic cross in Clonmacnois when they met the American again. He had not only seen everything Russell and Jane had recommended, but he had managed to visit his relatives in Limerick as well. Jane and Russell felt Ireland in four days was something of a record!

Around the world in 20 days

Vocabulary			Wortschatz
35	Head of State	'hed əv 'steɪt	Staatsoberhaupt
	particularly	pə'tɪkjʊləlɪ	insbesondere, besonders
	monument	'mɒnjʊmənt	Denkmal
	relics	'relɪks	Reste, Andenken
	Stone Age	'stəʊn eɪdʒ	Steinzeitalter
	to inhabit	tʊ ɪn'hæbɪt	bewohnen, wohnen, leben in
	tribe	traɪb	(Volks-)Stamm
	to reach	tə 'ri:tʃ	erreichen, erlangen
	in the pre-Christian era	ɪn ðə 'pri:'krɪstʃən 'ɪərə	in vorchristlicher Zeit
	era	'ɪərə	Zeit(alter)
	Celtic	'keltɪk	keltisch, das Keltische
	Irish	'aɪərɪʃ	irisch, das Irische
	saint	seɪnt	Heiliger
	Christianity	krɪstɪ'ænətɪ	Christentum
	innovation	ɪnəʊ'veɪʃn	Neuerung
	monastery	'mɒnəstrɪ	Kloster
	to centre	tə 'sentə	kreisen, sich drehen um, sich konzentrieren
	monk	mʌŋk	Mönch
	to illustrate	tʊ 'ɪləstreɪt	illustrieren, bebildern
	manuscript	'mænjʊskrɪpt	Handschrift, Manuskript
	to be on display	tə bɪ ɒn dɪ'spleɪ	ausgestellt sein
	to settle	tə 'setl	sich niederlassen
	round tower	raʊnd 'taʊə	Rundturm
	to arrive on the scene	tʊ ə'raɪv ɒn ðə 'si:n	auftauchen
	kingdom	'kɪŋdəm	Königreich
	occupation	ɒkjʊ'peɪʃn	Besetzung
	profound	prə'faʊnd	tief(greifend), gründlich, schwerwiegend
	occupant	'ɒkjʊpənt	Besetzer, Bewohner
	feudal system	'fju:dl sɪstəm	Feudalsystem, Lehnswesen
	to grant	tə 'grɑ:nt	übertragen, zugestehen, gewähren
	in return	ɪn rɪ'tɜ:n	als Gegenleistung, dafür
	to rule	tə 'ru:l	(be)herrschen
	Reformation	refə'meɪʃn	Reformation
	to remain	tə rɪ'meɪn	bleiben
	famine	'fæmɪn	Hungersnot
	starvation	stɑ:'veɪʃn	Hungertod
	to emigrate	tʊ 'emɪgreɪt	auswandern
	to intensify	tʊ ɪn'tensɪfaɪ	verstärken
	anti-Irish	'æntɪ 'aɪərɪʃ	anti-irisch
	reaction	rɪ'ækʃn	Reaktion, Verhalten
	Easter Rising	'i:stə 'raɪzɪŋ	Osteraufstand

	to proclaim	tə prə'kleɪm	verkünden
	provisional government	prə'vɪʒnəl 'gʌvənmənt	Übergangsregierung, provisorische Regierung
	partition	pɑː'tɪʃn	Teilung
	county	'kaʊntɪ	Grafschaft
	Protestant	'prɒtɪstənt	protestantisch
35 A	tour	tʊə	Rundreise
	to keep	tə 'kiːp	behalten
	to go ahead	tə gəʊ ə'hed	anfangen, weitermachen
	Irish whiskey	'aɪərɪʃ 'wɪskɪ	irischer Whiskey (*Gegensatz:* Scotch whisky = schottischer Whisky)
	spoonful	'spuːnfʊl	ein Löffelvoll
	cream	kriːm	Sahne
	to pronounce	tə prə'naʊns	aussprechen
	relatives	'relətɪvz	Verwandte
	great-great-grandfather	'greɪtgreɪt'grændfɑːðə	Ururgroßvater
	distant	'dɪstənt	entfernt
	elder	'eldə	älter(e)
	Tourist Office	'tʊərɪst ɒfɪs	Fremdenverkehrsverein
	brochure	'brəʊʃə	Broschüre
	plenty	'plentɪ	viel(e)
	protection	prə'tekʃn	Schutz
	riches	'rɪtʃɪz	Reichtum, Schätze
	gold	gəʊld	Gold
	silver	'sɪlvə	Silber
	day-trip	'deɪtrɪp	Tagesausflug
	prehistoric	priːhɪ'stɒrɪk	prähistorisch
	to be worth	tə bɪ 'wɜːθ	wert sein, sich lohnen
	the day after tomorrow	ðə 'deɪ ɑːftə tə'mɒrəʊ	übermorgen
	cross	krɒs	Kreuz
	I must be off now	aɪ məs bɪ 'ɒf naʊ	ich muß jetzt gehen
	Scriptures	'skrɪptʃəz	die Heilige Schrift
	hi!	haɪ	hallo! (guten) Tag!
	guy *(AE)*	gaɪ	Kerl, Bursche
	record	'rekɔːd	Rekord
35 B	patron saint	'peɪtrən 'seɪnt	Schutzpatron, Schutzheiliger
35 C	Tourist Board	'tʊərɪst bɔːd	Fremdenverkehrsbüro
35 D	purpose	'pɜːpəs	Zweck, Absicht
35 F	Common Market	'kɒmən 'mɑːkɪt	Gemeinsamer Markt, Europäische Gemeinschaft
35 I	punt	pʌnt	Irisches Pfund *(Währung)*
	to issue	tʊ 'ɪʃuː	(her)ausgeben, in Umlauf setzen
35 J	Gaelic	'geɪlɪk	gälisch, das Gälische

	constitution	kɒnstɪˈtjuːʃn	Verfassung
	related to	rɪˈleɪtɪd tʊ	verwandt mit
35 K	contribution	kɒntrɪˈbjuːʃn	Beitrag
	literature	ˈlɪtrətʃə	Literatur
	author	ˈɔːθə	Autor
	writer	ˈraɪtə	Schriftsteller
	to defend	tə dɪˈfend	verteidigen
	dean	diːn	Dekan
	cathedral	kəˈθiːdrəl	Kathedrale, Dom
	wit	wɪt	Geist, Witz, witziger Kopf
	playwright	ˈpleɪraɪt	Stückeschreiber
	importance	ɪmˈpɔːtns	Bedeutung
	earnest	ˈɜːnɪst	ernst; aufrichtig, ehrlich
	superman	ˈsuːpəmæn	Übermensch
	Nobel Prize	nəʊbel ˈpraɪz	Nobelpreis
	legend	ˈledʒənd	Legende, Sage, Märchen
	novelist	ˈnɒvəlɪst	Romanschriftsteller
35 M	neither of them	ˈnaɪðər əv ðəm	keine(r) von beiden
	talkative	ˈtɔːkətɪv	redselig
	to ask for advice	tʊ ˈɑːsk fər ədˈvaɪs	um Rat fragen
	brother-in-law	ˈbrʌðərɪnlɔː	Schwager

35

UNIT 36

CB Nowadays you can't go anywhere without seeing advertisements – in buses, in the Underground, on street hoardings, in newspapers and magazines. Advertisements on radio and television are called commercials. In Britain, the BBC (British Broadcasting Corporation), which is a non-profitmaking public company, doesn't broadcast any advertising whatever. It gets its money from the government. The second television network, the IBA (Independent Broadcasting Authority), gets its money from advertising. Firms pay a lot of money to advertise their products on television.
The new cable television networks get their money in other ways.
In the United States, the different private television networks sell their broadcasting time to sponsors who buy or produce programmes and often interrupt them for commercials.

36 A To buy or not to buy

(J = Jane, R = Russell)

R Good morning! Mrs Egan?
J Yes.
R Have you got a moment, Mrs Egan?
J Well – what do you want?
R My name's Russell Grant. I'm from "Wonderhelp" – kitchen and household equipment.
J I see. No, I'm sorry, I've got a lot of housework to do.
R Ah, I've got the very thing you need. If you could spare me a few moments now, I could save you a lot of time!
J I see – you want to sell me something.
R Sell you something? No, Mrs Egan, I'm going to give you something! I've got some free samples here for you to try out.
J Well, all right, I'll have them if they're free.

R Very wise, Mrs Egan. I've got two different brands of washing powder for you to try.
"Washo washes whiter!"
I'm sure you've seen the advertisements for "Washo" on television – five million housewives can't be wrong!

J I'm not so sure about that.
None of my friends use it. They all find it too expensive.
"Washo washes whiter."
Washo washes whiter than what?

R "Washo washes whiter than white!"

J Well, it's easy for you to say that, but I don't believe it.

R Plenty of people believe it!
I've sold this washing powder to lots of housewives, and every one of them has been satisfied with it.

J What about the other brand of washing powder you mentioned?

R "Splendo" – for perfect whiteness!

J Hmm. "For perfect whiteness".
So "Splendo" is better than "Washo"?
Or are they both the same?

R Well, there's little difference between them. But I can assure you that they're both excellent.

J They're exactly the same!
They each have exactly the same ingredients! Do they cost the same?

R No, "Washo" is a little cheaper than "Splendo", because "Splendo" has an extra whiteness guarantee – see, here it is, on the side of the packet.
But very few of our customers notice that they're the same. We sell a great deal of both brands.

J Well, there are a lot of people who don't read the small print. There aren't many people who are critical enough.

R Quite right, Mrs Egan, quite right!
It's a pity there aren't more people like you! Now, I've got something else for you to look at – "Easiwipe", the wonder shoe-cleaner! It cleans your shoes all by itself! No rubbing, no brushing! I've got a special offer here for you to test.

J Cleans your shoes all by itself?

R That's right!
(J puts a tube of shoe-cleaner and a pair of shoes on the table and waits.)

R Er, are you all right, Mrs Egan?

J "Easiwipe cleans your shoes all by itself."
That was what you said, wasn't it?

R Yes, that's right.

J Well why isn't it cleaning my shoes then?

R Well, we don't mean it quite like that. Naturally you have to put it on the shoes. But you only need a little, so it saves you a lot of work – and a lot of time!

J But it costs a lot – it won't save me much money. No, I'm quite happy with normal shoe polish, thank you.

R Ah, well why not get your husband something for the car? Look – "Wonderwax" – "It cleans your car . . ."

J ". . . cleaner than clean!"

R Exactly, Mrs Egan! So you've seen our advertisements on television?

J Yes – I bought some "Wonderwax" for my husband a few weeks ago and it's no good at all. It doesn't clean the car, and it's very expensive.
There are lots of different brands of car wax like this, and none of them are any good. They're all useless.

R I'm sure very few people would agree with you there, Mrs Egan.
Did you follow the instructions?

J Well, they were too difficult for my husband to follow. The car looked awful.

36

R Perhaps you didn't use the right cloth to polish the car with? Every housewife should have one of our "Supershine" polishing cloths – only 88 pence each!

J No, I'm sorry, I've got plenty of polishing cloths, thank you. Look, I'm awfully sorry, but I've got a lot of housework to do, I really can't spare the time.
I don't normally buy things at the door anyway.

R May I leave you a free sample of "Buzzoff", the new wonder fly-killer?

J No, I'm sorry, I'm really very busy. Goodbye.

R Well, it's been a pleasure to talk to you, Mrs Egan. Goodbye.

(R tries to start his car, but it won't start. He comes back.)

J Oh, it's you again!

R I'm very sorry to trouble you, Mrs Egan. Could I ask you a favour?

J Yes, what is it?

R Could I possibly use your phone for a moment?
I'm having a little trouble with my car.
I think the electrical system's got wet.
It happens every time it rains.

J You need "Wonderstart", the motorist's friend! Gives your engine a new start! Just spray it on and your car starts at once! None of my friends would ever be without it.

R Oh, I say, that sounds good!

J Only 88 pence! And I can make you a special offer, too – a free hand-wiping cloth with every can!

R I'll take it!
But tell me, Mrs Egan, don't you need it yourself?

J No, I've got plenty, thank you.
My husband's a sales representative – he's the local agent for "Wonderstart". He sells lots of it.

R Thank you very much, Mrs Egan, I'm awfully grateful – you've saved me a great deal of time!

36 B Questions

What's Russell's job in the story?
Who's Russell's employer?
What did Jane buy for her husband a few weeks ago?
What does the word "brand" mean in the context of the story?
Why did Russell come back again?
Where can you see advertisements? (Give three possibilities.)
Does the BBC get its money from advertising?

36 C And you?

Do you buy the products that are advertised on television, in the Underground or elsewhere?
Can you think of a good advertisement that tries to persuade people to buy something?

a) much / many – a lot (of) / lots (of) / plenty (of)

How **much** money have you got?	*Wieviel Geld ...*
He hasn't got **many** friends.	*.... nicht viele Freunde*
There aren't **many** people who are critical enough.	*.... nicht viele Leute*
He's got **plenty of** articles but he doesn't sell many.	*.... eine Menge*
The salesman talks **a lot.**	*.... viel*

"Much" steht bei einer unbestimmten Menge, also vor nicht zählbaren Substantiven.
"Many" steht bei zählbaren Substantiven.
Im gesprochenen Englisch verwendet man "much" bzw. "many" überwiegend in verneinten Sätzen und in Fragesätzen. In bejahten Sätzen stehen anstelle von "much" und "many" Umschreibungen wie "a lot (of)", "lots (of)", "plenty (of)", "a great deal (of)".
Ausnahmen: In der Schriftsprache sowie nach "too", "so", "as" und "very" können "much" und "many" auch in bejahenden Sätzen stehen, z. B.: That was too much for him. We had so much fun on our tour of Wales. Thank you very much.

b) little / a little – few / a few

There's **very little** difference.	*sehr wenig*
This washing powder is **a little** cheaper than that one.	*etwas*
Very few people would agree with you.	*sehr wenige*
Could you spare me **a few** moments?	*einige*

Merken Sie sich diese kleinen Wörter "little", "a little", "few" und "a few" gut, denn sie werden häufig gebraucht. "Little" und "few" werden häufig mit "very" verstärkt. "A few" bedeutet soviel wie "some".
Ein kleines Problem hinsichtlich der Unterscheidung von "little" und "few" besteht bei der Steigerung. Selbst Engländer zögern, ob sie "less" oder "fewer" sagen sollen: There were less (fewer) people at the demonstration. Eigentlich heißt es "fewer people", denn "people" ist zählbar. Natürlich wird "less people" genauso akzeptiert.

36

36 E Put in "much", "many", "little", "a little", "few", "a few" or "a lot of": ○○

How ..... does that car wax cost?
We're staying in Brighton for ..... days.
May I have ..... more milk, please?
I haven't ..... time for playing tennis.
There are ..... fine shops in London.
Have you read ..... books so far this year?
There were only ..... people in the restaurant.
How ..... chairs are there in this room?
There's very ..... sugar in my tea.
I've had ..... trouble with my car this morning.
..... firms pay ..... money to advertise their products on television.
There's only very ..... bread in the house.

36 F all / none

There are a number of boxes. **All** of them are empty.	*alle*
None of them are (is) full.	*keine*

Nach "all" im Sinne von *alle* steht das Verb im Plural.
Nach "none" steht das Verb je nach Betrachtungsweise entweder im Plural oder im Singular.
Wenn es sich nur um zwei Dinge handelt, können wir sagen: **Both** of them are empty. **Neither** of them is full.
Nach "neither" *(kein, -e, -er von beiden)* steht das Verb immer im Singular.

36 G each / every / either / any — jede(-r,-s)

Each Common Market country . . .	*Jedes der EG-Länder . . .*
Every country has got its problems.	*Jedes Land (der Erde) . . .*
She's wearing a ring on **either/each** hand.	*. . . an jeder Hand.*
You can get **any** book you like.	*. . . jedes beliebige . . .*

Mit "each" wählt man aus einer begrenzten Anzahl aus, mit "every" bezeichnet man die Gesamtheit. Es kommt jedoch auch vor, daß "each" und "every" gleichbedeutend verwendet werden: You look more beautiful each (every) time I see you.

He knows each of them. He knows every one of them.	*Er kennt jede(n) von ihnen.*

"Each of" ist gleichbedeutend mit "every one of", *jede(r) einzelne* aus einer begrenzten Anzahl.
"Either" bedeutet *jede(-r,-s) von zweien.*
"Any" bedeutet *jede(-r,-s) beliebige, ganz gleich welche(-r,-s).*

36 H Complete the sentences with "each", "every", "everybody" or "either": ⌓⌓

Would . . . . listen, please?
Jane goes to work . . . . . morning.
These shirts cost £15 . . . .
Has . . . . of your parents visited you?
They seem to be afraid of . . . . other.
Jane and Russell see . . . . . other . . . . day.
You can come on Monday or Tuesday, ... day is fine.

a)		Objekt 1	Objekt 2
	Humphrey gave	Graham him	the letter.
		Objekt 2	Objekt 1
	Humphrey gave	the letter it	to Graham. (and to nobody else) to him.

Folgende Verben können wie "give" verwendet werden: bring, hand, leave, offer, pay, play, promise, read, recommend, sell, send, show, take, tell, write.
Nach diesen Verben kann das indirekte Objekt (O 1) ohne "to" vor dem direkten Objekt (O 2) stehen oder, wenn es besonders betont werden soll, mit "to" an das direkte Objekt (O 2) angeschlossen werden.

b)		O 2	O 1
	I'll introduce	you	to Jane. to her.

Nach folgenden Verben wird das indirekte Objekt (O 1) immer mit "to" angeschlossen: address, describe, explain, introduce, mention, point out, propose, report, return, say, speak, suggest.

c)		O 1	O 2
	Jane bought	her husband	a tie.
		O 2	O 1
	Jane bought	a tie	for her husband.

Nach folgenden Verben wird, wenn das indirekte Objekt (O 1) nachgestellt wird, mit "for" angeschlossen: build, buy, choose, find, get, make, order, paint, reserve, type, win.
Bei den Verben "bring", "leave" und "play" kann das indirekte Objekt sowohl mit "for" als auch mit "to" angeschlossen werden.

d)		O 1	O 2
	Graham asked	Humphrey him	a question.

Nach den Verben "ask", "cost", "forgive", "refuse" kann das indirekte Objekt nicht mit "to" oder "for" nachgestellt werden.

36 J Complete the sentences: ○○

Graham explained . . . . . everything . . . . . his students.
Russell asked . . . Jane a lot of questions . . . . about the car.
We paid . . . . . him a visit.
Humphrey reported . . . . . the accident . . . . . the police.
Jane sent . . . . . her friends . . . . . some picture postcards.
Jane made . . . . . a steak . . . . . us.
Why didn't you introduce . . . . me . . . all your friends?
Are you writing this letter . . . . . your brother?
Show it . . . . . me.

36 K for + object + infinitive

I've got some free samples **for you to try out.**	*Ich habe einige Muster für Sie zum Ausprobieren.*
The instructions were too difficult **for my husband to follow.**	*Die Anweisungen waren für meinen Mann zu schwierig (zu schwer verständlich), als daß er sie hätte befolgen können.*

Nach "for" steht sehr häufig nicht nur ein Objekt, sondern eine Objekt + Infinitivkonstruktion.

36 L Translate the sentences:

Have you got a newspaper for me to read?
They've arranged for you to get our new brochure about Ireland.
The best thing for us to do is to go there ourselves.
I'm anxious for the painting to be ready on time.
The parcel is too heavy for you to lift.

36 M Situation – Say it in English

Fragen Sie jemanden, ob er einen Augenblick für Sie Zeit hat.
Ihr Gesprächspartner möchte wissen, worum es sich handelt.
Sagen Sie, daß Sie ein paar Muster für ihn zum Ausprobieren haben.
Versichern Sie Ihrem Gesprächspartner, daß diese Artikel ausgezeichnet sind.
Ihr Gesprächspartner bezweifelt das.
Er fragt, woher Sie das wissen.
Sagen Sie, daß Sie ihm ein Sonderangebot machen können.

36 N Summary

Mrs Egan was busy doing her housework when the doorbell rang. It was a door-to-door salesman who had a lot of household products to offer. He wanted to sell Mrs Egan his company's wonder washing powder "Washo". But he found an extremely critical consumer in Mrs Egan, who quickly made him admit that there was not really much difference between his washing powder and all the others.
He had equally little success when he showed her his shoe-cleaner, car wax and special polishing cloths. Finally Mrs Egan decided she had wasted enough time and sent the poor salesman away. A few minutes later, however, he returned and asked if he could use her phone. He was unable to start his car and wanted to ring a garage. But he didn't need to. Mrs Egan gave him a can of "Wonderstart" for the engine and convinced him of the quality of this product. The salesman realised why she had been so critical. Her husband was also a salesman and she knew all about selling methods.

To be or not to be

Vocabulary			Wortschatz
36	hoarding	ˈhɔ:dɪŋ	Reklametafel, -fläche
	commercials	kəˈmɜ:ʃls	Funk-, Fernsehwerbung
	non-profitmaking	nɒn ˈprɒfɪtmeɪkɪŋ	nicht auf Gewinn ausgerichtet
	to broadcast	tə ˈbrɔ:dkɑ:st	ausstrahlen, senden
	network	ˈnetwɜ:k	(Sende-)Netz
	product	ˈprɒdʌkt, ˈprɒdəkt	Produkt, Erzeugnis
	cable television	ˈkeɪbl telɪvɪʒn	Kabelfernsehen
	sponsor	ˈspɒnsə	Geldgeber, Förderer
36 A	housework	ˈhaʊswɜ:k	Hausarbeit
	free sample	fri: ˈsɑ:mpl	(Waren-)Probe, Muster
	wise	waɪz	klug, weise
	brand	brænd	Marke, Sorte; Warenzeichen
	powder	ˈpaʊdə	Pulver
	housewife, pl housewives	ˈhaʊswaɪf, ˈhaʊswaɪvz	Hausfrau(en)
	satisfied with	ˈsætɪsfaɪd ˈwɪð	zufrieden mit
	to assure	tʊ əˈʃʊə	versichern
	ingredients	ɪnˈgri:djənts	Bestandteile, Zutaten
	guarantee	gærənˈti:	Garantie
	a great deal of	ə ˈgreɪt ˈdi:l əv	eine Menge, recht, sehr viel
	small print	ˈsmɔ:l ˈprɪnt	Kleindruck, das Kleingedruckte
	critical	ˈkrɪtɪkl	kritisch
	shoe-cleaner	ˈʃu:kli:nə	Schuhputzmittel
	to clean	tə ˈkli:n	putzen, reinigen
	to rub	tə ˈrʌb	reiben, scheuern
	to brush	tə ˈbrʌʃ	bürsten
	to test	tə ˈtest	ausprobieren
	naturally	ˈnætʃrəlɪ	natürlich, selbstverständlich
	shoe polish	ˈʃu: pɒlɪʃ	Schuhcreme
	wax	wæks	Wachs
	useless	ˈju:sləs	nutzlos
	instructions	ɪnˈstrʌkʃnz	(Gebrauchs-)Anweisung
	cloth	klɒθ	Tuch
	to polish	tə ˈpɒlɪʃ	(auf)polieren
	fly-killer	ˈflaɪkɪlə	Fliegentötungsmittel
	pleasure	ˈpleʒə	Vergnügen
	to trouble	tə ˈtrʌbl	stören, belästigen
	to spray	tə ˈspreɪ	aufsprühen
	to wipe	tə ˈwaɪp	(auf)wischen
	hand-wiping cloth	ˈhændwaɪpɪŋ klɒθ	Wischtuch
	can	kæn	Dose, Büchse
	sales representative	ˈseɪlz reprɪzentətɪv	(Handels-)Vertreter

36 B	employer	ɪm'plɔɪə	Arbeitgeber
	context	'kɒntekst	Zusammenhang
	trademark	'treɪdmɑ:k	Waren-, Gütezeichen
	to distinguish	tə dɪ'stɪŋgwɪʃ	unterscheiden
36 C	elsewhere	els'weə	anderswo
	to persuade s.b.	tə pə'sweɪd	jdn. überreden
36 E	to advertise	tʊ 'ædvətaɪz	*hier:* werben, Reklame machen; *auch:* inserieren, eine Anzeige aufgeben
36 L	I'm anxious	aɪm 'æŋkʃəs	ich mache mir Sorgen, bin besorgt
36 N	salesman	'seɪlzmən	Verkäufer, Vertreter
	consumer	kən'sju:mə	Verbraucher
	to admit	tʊ əd'mɪt	zugeben, zugestehen
	equally	'i:kwəlɪ	gleich, ebenso, genauso
	success	sək'ses	Erfolg
	garage	'gærɑ:ʒ	Reparaturwerkstätte, Tankstelle, Garage
	to convince s.b.	tə kən'vɪns	jdn. überzeugen
	selling methods	'selɪŋ meθədz	Verkaufsmethoden

36

Aus: ON THE WAY 2 (Englisch für die Erwachsenenbildung), Ernst Klett Verlag, Stuttgart 1993

UNIT 37

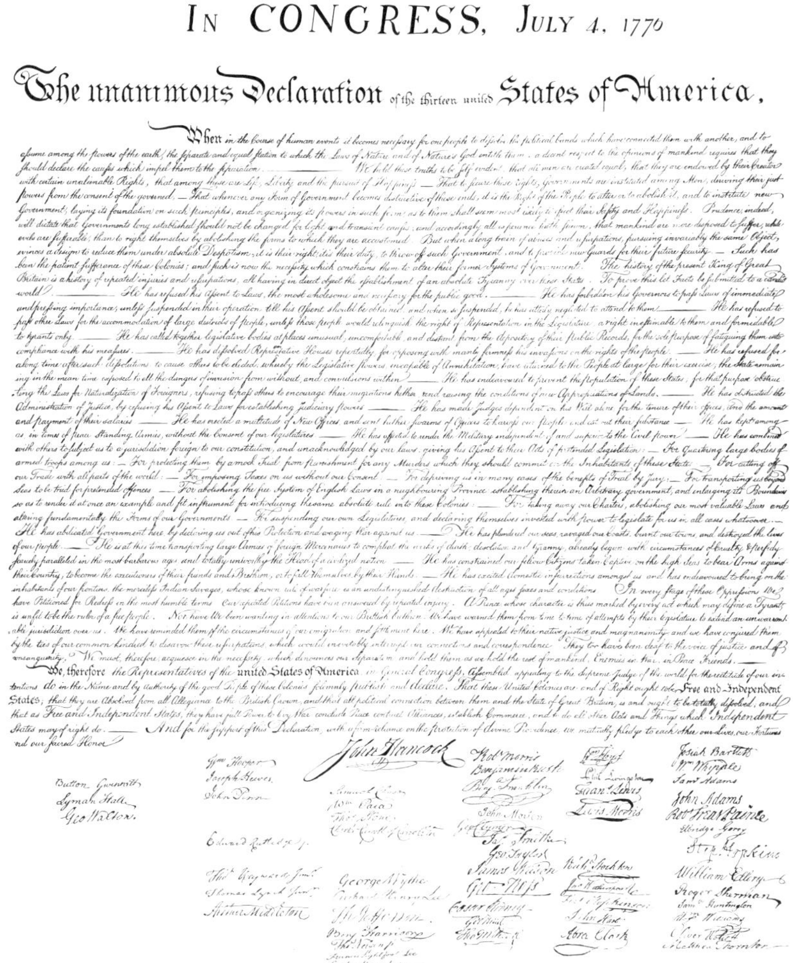

IN CONGRESS, JULY 4, 1776.

The unanimous Declaration of the thirteen united States of America,

When in the Course of human events, it becomes necessary for one people to dissolve the political bands which have connected them with another, and to assume among the powers of the earth, the separate and equal station to which the Laws of Nature and of Nature's God entitle them, a decent respect to the opinions of mankind requires that they should declare the causes which impel them to the separation. — We hold these truths to be self-evident, that all men are created equal, that they are endowed by their Creator with certain unalienable Rights, that among these are Life, Liberty and the pursuit of Happiness. — That to secure these rights, Governments are instituted among Men, deriving their just powers from the consent of the governed, — That whenever any Form of Government becomes destructive of these ends, it is the Right of the People to alter or to abolish it, and to institute new Government, laying its foundation on such principles and organizing its powers in such form, as to them shall seem most likely to effect their Safety and Happiness. Prudence, indeed, will dictate that Governments long established should not be changed for light and transient causes; and accordingly all experience hath shewn, that mankind are more disposed to suffer, while evils are sufferable, than to right themselves by abolishing the forms to which they are accustomed. But when a long train of abuses and usurpations, pursuing invariably the same Object evinces a design to reduce them under absolute Despotism, it is their right, it is their duty, to throw off such Government, and to provide new Guards for their future security. — Such has been the patient sufferance of these Colonies; and such is now the necessity which constrains them to alter their former Systems of Government. The history of the present King of Great Britain is a history of repeated injuries and usurpations, all having in direct object the establishment of an absolute Tyranny over these States. To prove this, let Facts be submitted to a candid world.

The Declaration of Independence

The first English settlement was established at Jamestown, Virginia, over a hundred years after Christopher Columbus's first voyage to America in 1492.

In 1620 the Pilgrim Fathers, who had sailed from Britain in the "Mayflower", landed in Plymouth Harbour on the Massachusetts coast.

From Jamestown and Plymouth a nation grew and spread westward. From the 1760's onwards, the thirteen English colonies rebelled against the mother country. In 1776 they declared their independence with the "Declaration of Independence", which was written by Thomas Jefferson. The thirteen separate "colonies" joined together in a loose confederation, with a Congress where state representatives discussed common problems.

In 1787 a convention met at Philadelphia to draw up a Constitution. George Washington became the first President of the United States. Two years later James Madison drew up ten amendments guaranteeing certain individual rights and liberties, such as freedom of speech, of the press and of religion, freedom to assemble peaceably etc. These amendments have become known as the "Bill of Rights". Within two centuries the new nation grew from thirteen to fifty states. It has become a mighty world power.

37 A In the museum ○○

(G = Guard, A = Visitor A, B = Visitor B, C = Visitor C, D = Visitor D, E = Visitor E, Voices, An = Announcement)

G Hi, there! How are you today? I'm Tracy, and I'm a security guard here at the Guggenheim Museum. It's a fantastic place, isn't it? It was designed by a famous architect, Frank Lloyd Wright about forty years ago. It's a great place. Well I think it is.

A Excuse me. Are you a guide?

G No, sir. We don't have guides in the museum. But you can buy a catalogue. They are sold in the bookshop, over there, by the entrance.

A Thanks a lot.

G You're welcome. Have a nice day. I'm asked a lot of questions. And right now there's a special exhibition. It's being held to . . .

(Another visitor interrupts her.)

B Hi, there! Can you tell me where the pictures are?

G They're here. Well, there, and there, and there.

B Gee! You don't say! Those aren't pictures.

G Yes, sir. They are. And they've been painted by famous artists . . .

B Come on! That's not a painting, is it?

G Er – no. I agree it's not a regular painting. But it's a fine work of art. It was made by a famous artist – Jay Splatsky. Splatsky's work is shown all over the world . . .

B Wow! Look at that, then!

G Beautiful, isn't it?

B Not exactly. But I can see the name of the artist, anyway. It was painted by Bertram J. Filbeck.

G No sir. I'm afraid you're wrong. Filbeck didn't paint it. It was painted by Splatsky's daughter, Bea Splatsky. Look!

B I don't get it. The name's written there. On the – er – picture.

G Yes, I know. It was painted for Mr Filbeck. But he never pays for his pictures. Well, he never pays cash. So Bea Splatsky painted this one specially for him. It's called "On credit".

B Who paid for it?

G Oh, no one paid for it. That's why it's called "On credit". It was given to the museum by the artist.

B Well, what d'you know!

G Excuse me. I'm being called on my radio.

(She listens to radio, then answers call.)

G Yes. Sure. I'll be there momentarily. I must go. One of the paintings has been damaged. (In another part of the museum, two visitors are standing by a portrait with a large hole in it.)

C What have you done to that painting? Look! It's ruined.

D I haven't touched the painting. It's always been like that. It was painted with a hole in it.

G Come on, come on! What's happening here?

C This picture has been damaged.

G Oh, that's all right. It was damaged last week. You see, people don't like it.
Don't worry. It's going to be restored.
Then it will be damaged again.
Most people don't like it.
I don't think I like it.
Not really.
Modern art is difficult, isn't it?
Some people like it very much.

Guggenheim Museum, New York

Voices Gee! Look at that!
Isn't that just great!
Cute, isn't it?
G Others aren't so sure.
Voices What do you think of that?
I don't know. It's kind of funny.
I agree. Do you know what it is?
I don't know. I wonder, is it a fish?
No. I don't think so. Maybe it's a frog.
G Some people argue about the paintings and sculpture . . .
Voices I like it! I like it!
No. It's awful.
Did we really pay to see this?
I shall insist on complaining to Mr Guggenheim personally.
You can't. Mr Guggenheim is dead.
Killed by one of his pictures, no doubt.
G And sometimes the pictures are damaged. And the police are called.
And people are arrested.
And, of course, some people don't come to look at the pictures.
But I have a job to do.
The pictures must be protected.

(To visitor E)
G Excuse me, sir. You can't take pictures out of the gallery. It's forbidden.
E I'm not taking the picture away.
It's being put back.
G Put back? I don't understand.
E It was stolen. I stole it.
But no one would buy it. No one!
Now I want to put it back.
G Ah! I get it! I always try to help.
What about here?
It could be hung here.
G This way up. It has to be hung like this.
E Oh, I see. No wonder people didn't like it the other way up. It looks quite nice now. Are you going to arrest me – for stealing the picture?
G Of course not. You've been taught a lesson. A lesson about art.
An Ladies and Gentlemen, the museum will be closed in two minutes.
G Well, it's the end of the day.
Oh, by the way, I'm a painter too.
These were painted by me.
I'm still working on this one.
It'll be finished soon.

Manhattan (New York)

37 B Questions

What do you understand by the "Mayflower"?
Who wrote the Declaration of Independence?
Name another important document in American history.
How many states has America got?
Who was Frank Lloyd Wright?

37 C And you?

Would you like to spend your holidays in the States? What cities would you like to see?
Do you like modern art?
Have you ever tried to paint yourself?
Who's your favourite painter?

37 D The Passive (Voice) (I) — Das Passiv

present simple:	I am (I'm) asked	*ich werde gefragt*
past simple:	I was asked	*ich wurde gefragt*
present perfect:	I have (I've) been asked	*ich bin gefragt worden*
past perfect:	I had (I'd) been asked	*ich war gefragt worden*
will-future:	I will (I'll) be asked	*ich werde gefragt werden*
future perfect:	I will (I'll) have been asked	*ich werde gefragt worden sein*
going-to-future:	I'm going to be asked	*ich werde gefragt werden*
infinitive:	to be asked	*gefragt werden*
perfect infinitive:	to have been asked	*gefragt worden sein*

Das Passiv wird mit "to be" und dem Partizip Perfekt gebildet. Eine Fehlerquelle bei der Bildung der englischen Passivformen ist das deutsche *werden*. Verwechseln Sie nicht: I'm asked, *ich werde gefragt* mit I'll ask, *ich werde fragen*.

37 E Complete the sentences using the correct form of the passive: ◯◯

Catalogues .... by the entrance. (sell, simple present)
The museum .... in 1959. (open, past perfect)
A special exhibition .... next month. (show, going-to-future)
Yesterday a picture .... (damage, simple past)
The police .... (call, simple past)
The painting .... (finish, soon, will-future)

37 F Use of the Passive — Verwendung des Passivs

active:	Frank Lloyd Wright (subject)	designed (active verb-form)	the Guggenheim Museum. (object)
passive:	The Guggenheim Museum (subject)	was designed (passive verb-form)	by Frank Lloyd Wright. (by + agent)

Im aktiven Satz handelt das Subjekt. Im Passivsatz geschieht dem Subjekt etwas. Der Inhalt dieser beiden Sätze ist derselbe. Es ändert sich nur die Blickrichtung.
Im aktiven Satz steht der Urheber im Zentrum. Im passiven Satz steht die Wirkung, das Ziel am Anfang und dann erst blicken wir zurück auf den Urheber (engl.: agent). Den Urheber kennzeichnen wir beim Passiv mit der Präposition "by". Ist der Urheber selbstverständlich, unwichtig oder unbekannt, lassen wir die Präposition "by" mit der Urheberangabe weg, z. B. The museum was opened in 1959.

37 G Translate the following sentences: OO

Die Sonderausstellung ist gestern eröffnet worden.
Ist Jane (schon) informiert worden?
Es wird alles bis zum 25. erledigt sein.
Wer soll (sollte) eingeladen werden?
Ich werde ihn nicht sehen.
Wann wurde das Haus gebaut?
Das Museum war am Montag geschlossen.
Das Museum wurde um 5 Uhr geschlossen.

Metropolitan Museum (New York)

37 H Famous museums in New York City (CB)

New York City is one of the world's great centres for culture and the arts. Cultural treasures can be found in every museum.
Today the Metropolitan Museum of Art, founded in 1870, is the largest art museum in the Western Hemisphere. Its collections include more than three million works of art, from ancient, medieval, and modern times and from all parts of the world.
The Museum of Modern Art was founded in 1929. The collections include masterpieces of modern art from about 1880 to the present.
The Solomon R. Guggenheim Museum, an architectural landmark designed by Frank Lloyd Wright, presents changing exhibitions of modern masters and younger artists. The collection left to the museum by Solomon R. Guggenheim includes works by Kandinsky, Klee, Chagall and many others.

37 I Vocabulary Practice

Find words in the text 37 H that mean the following:

to establish
something made with very great skill
to plan
a person who produces paintings, drawings or other works of art
a highly valued object
to show

37 J US Money (CB)

The $ notes (AE: bills) are
$1, $5, $10, $20, $50, $100.
All notes are exactly
the same green colour and size.
There are 100 cents to the dollar.
The coins are: 1 cent, known as a penny
5 cents, known as a nickel
10 cents, known as a dime
25 cents, known as a quarter.
There are also half-dollar coins and you may even come across a dollar coin.

In the USA credit cards are widely used. In a hotel or restaurant you'll be asked: "Cash or charge?" You can pay cash or with "plastic money". You'll need to show some ID (= identification) when charging a purchase.
US dollar traveller's cheques can be used like cash. Shops, restaurants and hotels will accept them and they are much safer than cash.

37 K Situation – Say it in English

Sagen Sie, daß es ein großartiger Raum ist.
Sagen Sie, daß die Bilder von van Gogh im zweiten Stock (AE!) gezeigt werden.
Sagen Sie, daß das ein wunderbares Kunstwerk ist.
Fragen Sie Ihren Gesprächspartner, was er von Picassos Bildern hält.
Sagen Sie, daß Ihnen die frühen Werke von Picasso gut gefallen.
Sagen Sie, daß Sie sich nichts aus diesen Zeichnungen machen.
Sagen Sie, daß Sie moderne Kunst nicht mögen.
Sagen Sie jemandem, daß Sie anderer Meinung sind.
Sagen Sie Ihrem Gesprächspartner, daß Sie verstehen, worauf er hinauswill.
Fragen Sie Ihren Gesprächspartner, ob er sicher weiß, daß das Museum montags geschlossen ist.

37 L Summary ⚇

Tracy is a security guard at the Guggenheim Museum, so naturally she is asked a lot of questions by visitors. She gives them explanations about the pictures and the other works of art. Suddenly she is called away by radio. In another part of the museum two visitors are quarrelling about a portrait with a large hole in it. Tracy tells them that it was damaged last week and that it is going to be restored soon.
While protecting the pictures she listens to the comments of the visitors. Some people like the paintings, others complain about them. Then she notices a man with a painting under his arm. She tells him it is forbidden to take pictures out of the museum. The man explains that he is bringing the picture back. He stole it but he couldn't sell it. Tracy hangs the painting back on the wall and the man suddenly realises why nobody would buy it – he had held it the wrong way up. At the end of the day Tracy lets out a secret: She's a painter too.

I'm the greatest

Vocabulary			**Wortschatz**
37	settlement	ˈsetlmənt	(An-)Siedlung, Niederlassung
	to establish	tʊ ɪˈstæblɪʃ	gründen, errichten
	voyage	ˈvɔɪɪdʒ	(weite See-, Fern-)Reise
	to sail	tə ˈseɪl	zur See fahren, auslaufen, in See stechen; segeln
	harbour	ˈhɑːbə	Hafen
	coast	kəʊst	Küste
	to grow	tə ˈgrəʊ	wachsen
	to spread, spread, spread	tə ˈspred, spred, spred	sich ausdehnen, sich ausbreiten
	westward	ˈwestwəd	westwärts, in westliche(r) Richtung
	onwards	ˈɒnwədz	von . . . an, nach vorne, vorwärts, weiter fortschreitend
	colony	ˈkɒlənɪ	Niederlassung, Kolonie
	to rebel	tə rɪˈbel	rebellieren, sich auflehnen
	independence	ɪndɪˈpendəns	Unabhängigkeit
	Declaration of Independence	dekləˈreɪʃn əv ɪndɪˈpendəns	Unabhängigkeitserklärung
	separate	ˈseprət	getrennt
	loose	luːs	lose
	confederation	kənfedəˈreɪʃn	Staatenbund, Bündnis

37

	congress	ˈkɒŋgres	Kongreß (in USA = Senat und Repräsentantenhaus)
	representative	reprɪˈzentətɪv	Vertreter
	common	ˈkɒmən	gemeinsam
	convention	kənˈvenʃn	Zusammenkunft, Tagung, Kongreß
	to draw up	tə drɔ: ˈʌp	ausarbeiten, abfassen, entwerfen
	amendment	əˈmendmənt	Verbesserung, Ergänzung(santrag)
	to guarantee	tə gærənˈti:	garantieren, gewährleisten
	certain	ˈsɜ:tn	bestimmt, gewiß
	individual	ɪndɪˈvɪdjʊəl	Einzel-, persönlich
	rights	raɪts	Rechte
	liberties	ˈlɪbətɪz	Freiheiten, (Vor-)Rechte
	freedom	ˈfri:dəm	Freiheit
	religion	rɪˈlɪdʒən	Religion
	to assemble	tʊ əˈsembl	versammeln, zusammenkommen
	peaceably	ˈpi:səblɪ	friedlich
	Bill of Rights	ˈbɪl əv ˈraɪts	verfassungsmäßig garantierte Grundrechte
	mighty	ˈmaɪtɪ	mächtig, stark, gewaltig
37 A	security	sɪˈkjʊərətɪ	Sicherheit, Schutz
	to design	tə dɪˈzaɪn	entwerfen, konstruieren
	architect	ˈɑ:kɪtekt	Architekt, Baumeister
	entrance	ˈentrəns	Eingang
	you're welcome	jɔ: ˈwelkəm	bitte sehr, gern geschehen, nichts zu danken
	exhibition	eksɪˈbɪʃn	Ausstellung
	You don't say!	jʊ dən ˈseɪ	Was Sie nicht sagen!, nicht möglich!
	to paint	tə ˈpeɪnt	malen
	artist	ˈɑ:tɪst	Künstler
	come on! *(slang)*	kʌm ˈɒn	Unsinn!
	painting	ˈpeɪntɪŋ	Bild, Gemälde
	to get *(colloq.)*	tə get	verstehen, „kapieren“
	on credit	ɒn ˈkredɪt	auf Kredit
	What d'you know!	ˈwɒtdjʊ ˈnəʊ	Was Sie nicht sagen!, Was du nicht sagst!
	momentarily	ˈməʊməntərɪlɪ	*(AE)* im Augenblick, sofort, *(BE)* flüchtig
	to damage	tə ˈdæmɪdʒ	beschädigen, zerstören
	to touch	tə ˈtʌtʃ	be-, anrühren
	to restore	tə rɪˈstɔ:	wiederherstellen
	cute	kju:t	nett, niedlich, putzig
	sculpture	ˈskʌlptʃə	Plastik, Bildhauerei
	to insist on	tʊ ɪnˈsɪst ɒn	bestehen auf
	dead	ded	tot

	killed	kɪld	getötet
	to protect	tə prə'tekt	schützen
	to forbid, forbade, forbidden	tə fə'bɪd, fə'bæd, fə'bɪdn	verbieten
	to put back	tə pʊt 'bæk	zurückbringen
	to hang, hung, hung	tə 'hæŋ, hʌŋ, hʌŋ	(auf)hängen
37 F	agent	'eɪdʒ(ə)nt	Urheber *(Grammatik)*
37 H	culture	'kʌltʃə	Kultur
	arts	ɑ:ts	(freie, angewandte) Kunst
	treasure	'treʒə	Schatz
	western	'westən	westlich
	hemisphere	'hemɪsfɪə	Hemisphäre, (Erd-)Halbkugel
	to include	tʊ ɪn'klu:d	einschließen
	medieval	medɪ'i:vl	mittelalterlich
	to found	tə 'faʊnd	gründen
	masterpiece	'mɑ:stəpi:s	Meisterwerk
	architectural	ɑ:kɪ'tektʃərəl	baulich, architektonisch
	landmark	'lændmɑ:k	Markstein
37 I	skill	skɪl	Geschick(lichkeit)
	drawing	'drɔ:ɪŋ	Zeichnung
	highly valued object	'haɪlɪ 'vælju:d 'ɒbdʒɪkt	äußerst wertvoller Gegenstand
37 J	nickel	'nɪkl	Fünfcentstück
	dime	daɪm	Zehncentstück
	quarter	'kwɔ:tə	Vierteldollar, Fünfundzwanzigcentstück
	charge	tʃɑ:dʒ	(Konto-)Belastung
	identification card	aɪdentɪfɪ'keɪʃn kɑ:d	Personalausweis, Kennkarte
	purchase	'pɜ:tʃəs	Kauf
	to charge a purchase	tə tʃɑ:dʒ ə 'pɜ:tʃəs	mit Kreditkarte einkaufen
	traveller's cheque	'trævləz tʃek	Reisescheck
	to accept	tʊ ək'sept	annehmen, einlösen
	safe	seɪf	sicher
37 L	explanation	eksplə'neɪʃn	Erklärung
	to quarrel about	tə 'kwɒrəl əbaʊt	streiten über
	comment	'kɒment	Kritik, Äußerung, Kommentar, Bemerkung
	to notice	tə 'nəʊtɪs	bemerken, wahrnehmen, beobachten
	to let out	tə let 'aʊt	preisgeben, herauslassen
	secret	'si:krət	Geheimnis

UNIT 38

New Orleans, French Quarter

CB At the beginning of the 18th century the French were busy exploring the vast area of the Mississippi River basin. They claimed it for France and called it Louisiana in honour of the French King Louis XIV. Louisiana was lost to Spain in 1762 and was given back to France forty years later. In 1803 Napoleon agreed to the famous "Louisiana Purchase" and sold the territory to the United States for 15 million dollars.

The French who had settled there in the 17th and 18th centuries left a rich heritage: the French and Creole languages, customs, laws, and beautiful houses with courtyards. New Orleans, Louisiana's main city, has kept much of this French atmosphere alive in the old French Quarter.

38 A What a way to run an airline

(J = Jane, R = Russell, B = Businessman, A = Agent, Operator)

WHEN YOU FLY EXPRESS AIRLINES, YOU ARRIVE ON TIME!
WHEN YOU FLY WITH US, YOU HAVE NOTHING TO WORRY ABOUT.
ALWAYS FLY EXPRESS!

B Not true! It's not true

J What isn't true?

B That poster. When you fly Express Airlines, you never arrive on time.

A Oh yes, you do, sir. It's a great airline even though it does have problems – sometimes.

R What kind of problems?

B You'll find out.

A Oh, you have nothing to worry about. We're very reliable. Even the President flies with us.

R The President of the United States?

A No, sir. The President of Express Airlines. Mr Hiram Flugheim.

B Don't believe her. She has to say these things because the airline pays her. Huh!

J Let's sit down before all the seats are taken.

B That's not difficult since we're the only people here.

(Jane to businessman)

J Do you travel a lot?

B Oh yes. Yes. I'm in the – er – travel business. I . . .

R Since you're in the travel business, you can help us. When does our flight arrive in Denver?

B When it isn't late, Flight 213 arrives in Denver at quarter of twelve.

R Er – eleven forty-five? But that's very soon.

J Yes. It's nearly eleven now.

B Right. Here in New Orleans it's nearly eleven o'clock Central Time. But it's only ten o'clock Mountain Time. And it's Mountain Time in Denver. They're one hour behind.

J Isn't it time to reserve our seats?

B Don't worry. When it's time to check in, the agent over there makes an announcement.

R I think she's going to make an announcement now.

A At this time we regret to announce a delay of two hours to Express Airlines Flight 212 to Denver. Excuse me. Flight 213.

B Even though she's reading it, she makes mistakes.

J Flight 213. That's us. Why is there a delay?

R I don't know. Maybe there's a delay because the weather's bad.

B No. There's a delay because you're flying Express Airlines. Don't say I didn't warn you. Huh!
(The businessman's moustache falls off.)

New Orleans, French Quarter

J Excuse me. Is this your moustache?

B Thank you, ma'am.
Well, although I'm wearing it, it's not really mine.

J Then why are you wearing it?

B Because I don't want people to know who I am.

J Oh, I see.

R Jane! Our hotel!

J Oh, yes! We promised to check in by one o'clock.

R Where are the telephones?
I'll ring the hotel.

B Ring? Oh! You mean you'll call the hotel?
Look! The telephones are over there.

R Thanks very much.

B You're welcome, sir.

R Stay there while I phone.

J All right.

B Since we're here, we might as well enjoy ourselves.

J How?

B We can watch television while we're waiting.

J I don't think I've got any change.

38

J Have you got any?
B Yes, I do. I have some change.
You put in 35 cents. A quarter and a dime.

R Oh dear! No change.
Hello.
Operator Good morning. This is Miss Wicks.
Can I help you?
R Er – I hope so. I want to call the Wayfarer Hotel, Denver, and I want to reverse the charge.
Operator Oh! You mean call collect.
Do you have the number?
R Yes. I've got it here. 800 – 733-4367.
Operator 800? Then it's a toll-free number.
You don't have to pay, sir. Just dial the number. And have a nice day, sir.

J Do they always show films like this?
B Express Airlines show old movies because they can't afford anything else.
J Even though it's old, I like it.
It makes me cry. Look!

(Russell rejoins them.)
B Any luck?
R Although I rang several times,
I couldn't get through.
The number was engaged.
B Engaged? Oh, you mean busy?
A As you're the only passengers on this flight, I'm not making another announcement.
But I'm sorry to say your flight has been cancelled.
B I'm not surprised. Express Airlines usually cancel their flights.
R Since it's such a bad airline, why do you fly Express?
B I have to.
R Why?
B Because I'm the President.
A Mr Flugheim! It's Mr Flugheim.
B Yes. And I intend to sell Express Airlines – if anyone will buy it.
(To Jane and Russell)
B And now shall we look at another old movie?

38 B Questions

Which river flows through Louisiana?
What was the "Louisiana Purchase"?
What's the largest city in Louisiana?
In which time zone is Louisiana?
Name a place in the States which has Mountain Time.
Why is Mr Flugheim wearing a false moustache?
Who is Mr Flugheim?

A Mississippi riverboat

38 C And you?

You meet an American on a flight from Munich to Cologne.
Work out a conversation with him.

I'm talking **and** Humphrey is listening.
He spoke politely **but** firmly.

Konjunktionen sind Bindewörter wie z. B. "and", "but", "because", "although" usw. Sie verbinden Satzteile oder Sätze miteinander.

a) Reason clauses — Kausalsätze

She has to say these things **because** the airline pays her.	*weil*
Since you're in the travel business, you can help us.	*da ja, nachdem*
As you're the only passengers on this flight, I'm not making another announcement.	*da*

Die Konjunktionen "because", "since" und "as" leiten Nebensätze des Grundes ein.

b) Concessive clauses — Konzessivsätze

(Al)though I rang several times, I couldn't get through.	*obwohl, obgleich*
It's a great airline **even though** it does have problems sometimes.	*obwohl, obgleich*

Die Konjunktionen "though", "although" und "even though" leiten einräumende, einschränkende Nebensätze ein.

c) Time clauses — Temporalsätze

Stay there **while** I phone.	*während*
When it's time to check in, the agent over there makes an announcement.	*wenn*
Let's sit down **before** all the seats are taken.	*ehe, bevor*
I'll ring **as soon as** I arrive.	*sobald*
Please remain seated **until** the plane has stopped.	*bis*
The passengers were offered drinks **after** the plane had taken off.	*nachdem*

Die Konjunktionen "while", "when", "before", "as soon as", "till" ("until"), "after" leiten Nebensätze der Zeit ein. Beachten Sie den Unterschied zwischen "when" (zeitliche Bedeutung) und "if" (Bedingung); im Deutschen hingegen steht in beiden Fällen *wenn*.

38 E Complete the sentences with a suitable conjunction: ΩΩ

Maybe there's a delay . . . . . the weather's bad.
. . . . . he's wearing a moustache, it's not really his.
We can watch television . . . . . we're waiting.
. . . . . it's such a bad airline, why do you fly Express?
. . . . . he comes, let me know.
Let's have a swim . . . . . we have dinner.
. . . . . it isn't late, Flight 213 arrives at a quarter to twelve (AE: at quarter of twelve).
. . . . . Louisiana had been given back to France, Napoleon sold it to the United States.
. . . . . he arrives, the band will play the National Anthem.

38 F Join the following sentences by using conjunctions:

We're looking forward to Easter. We're going away for a few days.
The courts are under water. We can't play tennis.
She was tired. She went to work.
I was out. He called.
The weather was fine. We decided to go for a walk.
He was hurt. He continued to play.
He couldn't come. He was ill.
I'll support your idea. I'm not convinced.

38 G Spelling **Rechtschreibung**

Differences between British English (BE) and American English (AE):

BE	AE
metre	meter
centre	center
theatre	theater
catalogue	catalog
colour	color
harbour	harbor
jewellery	jewelry
traveller	traveler
cancelled	canceled
dialled	dialed

Die im BE üblichen Endungen -re bzw. -our werden im amerikanischen Englisch häufig zu -er bzw. -or.
Die Verdoppelung des -l- fällt im Amerikanischen meist weg.

38 H Is it British or American English?

Make a cross in the correct column:	BE	AE
Catalogs are sold over there.		
Yesterday I went to the theatre.		
The cars blocked the city centre.		
He dialed the wrong number.		
The flight was cancelled.		
There are a hundred centimeters in a meter.		
They do have some superb jewelry in Diamond Row.		
Free concerts are held frequently at Lincoln Center's Library of the Performing Arts.		

38 I Times and dates

There are four different time zones in the States:
Eastern Standard, Central, Mountain and Pacific Time.

San Francisco	Denver	New Orleans	New York
8 a.m. Pacific Time	9 a.m. Mountain Time	10 a.m. Central Time	11 a.m. Eastern Standard Time

What's the time?

BE:	It's (a) quarter to six.
AE:	It's quarter of six. (= before)

Dates are written differently from the way they are written in Britain.
3/18/83 means: March 18, 1983

38 J Flight announcements ◯◯

Flight 213 to Denver is now boarding.
This is the final call for Flight 213 to Denver. This flight is now closing at Gate 24.

Where was this announcement made?
a) in the plane before take-off
b) after the plane had taken off
c) in the airport lounge

Captain Redford and his crew welcome you on board EA service to Washington National Airport. Please fasten your seat belts and make sure that your seats are in an upright position for take-off. Please don't smoke until the no-smoking signs have been switched off.

What was the announcement about?
a) the final call for EA flight to Washington
b) a welcome on board and normal safety precautions
c) a delay of your flight

Good evening folks. This is your captain speaking. We'll shortly be landing at Moissant International Airport, New Orleans. Please extinguish your cigarettes and make sure that your seats are in an upright position. Please remain seated until the plane has come to a standstill and the engines are switched off. Thank you for flying Express Airlines. We hope you enjoyed the flight.

When did the captain make the announcement?
a) after landing
b) before landing
c) as the passengers get off

38 K Making telephone calls in the USA (CB)

The American telephone network is run by private companies. American telephone numbers are normally in this form: (212) 505-3896. The figures in brackets stand for the area code, 212 for example stands for New York. Many hotels, airline offices and other business services have "toll-free numbers" with an 800 prefix, e. g. 800/123-7906. The call doesn't cost you anything if the number you want starts with 800. For a long-distance call you can dial 0 and ask the operator to connect you or you dial the call yourself. A transfer-charge or reversed-charge call is known in the USA as a "collect call" or "call collect" *(R-Gespräch)*. If a number is engaged, Americans say it's "busy".

38 L Situation – Say it in English

Sagen Sie, daß Sie ein Ferngespräch nach San Francisco führen möchten.
Fragen Sie, wann Ihr Flug in Denver ankommt.
Fragen Sie, warum der Flug 213 nach Denver Verspätung hat.
Sie rufen in einem Hotel an. Sagen Sie, daß Sie für morgen abend ein Einzelzimmer reservieren möchten.
Ihre Gesprächspartnerin antwortet, daß sie ausgebucht sind, weil zur Zeit eine Industriemesse (industrial fair) stattfindet.
Fragen Sie, ob sie Ihnen ein anderes Hotel empfehlen kann.
Sagen Sie, daß die Telefonnummer immer besetzt war, obwohl Sie es mehrere Male probiert haben.
Sagen Sie, daß Sie beabsichtigen, nächstes Jahr nach New York zu fahren.

38 M Summary

Russell and Jane are at the airport in New Orleans. They've booked a flight to Denver with Express Airlines. Although they're early, they're the only people waiting for the flight. A stranger – a businessman with a false moustache – tells them that when you fly Express Airlines, you're always late. An airline agent hears this and says that Express Airlines are a great airline, even though they have problems. She says that even the President flies Express – she means the President of Express Airlines, not the President of the United States. There's an announcement over the loudspeakers that Jane and Russell's flight has been delayed. Russell reminds Jane that they'd promised to check in at their hotel in Denver by one o'clock, and goes to find a phone. Meanwhile, Jane and the businessman watch an old film on a pay television. Russell can't get through to the hotel. Then the airline agent comes across to tell them that their flight has been cancelled. Although Express Airlines are so bad, the businessman has to fly with them because he's the President of the airline – he's wearing a false moustache because he doesn't want to be recognised by his employees.

Come fly with me

Vocabulary			**Wortschatz**
38	to explore	tʊ ɪk'splɔː	erforschen, auskundschaften
	vast	vɑːst	weit, ausgedehnt
	river basin	'rɪvə beɪsn	Fluß-, Stromgebiet; Bucht, Hafenbecken
	to claim	tə 'kleɪm	fordern, Anspruch erheben
	in honour of	ɪn 'ɒnər əv	zu Ehren von
	heritage	'herɪtɪdʒ	Erbe, Erbschaft
	Creole	'kriːəʊl	(Adj) kreolisch; (S) Kreole, Kreolin
	custom	'kʌstəm	Sitte, Brauch(tum)
	law	lɔː	Gesetz
	courtyard	'kɔːtjɑːd	Hof
	main	meɪn	Haupt-
	alive	ə'laɪv	am Leben, lebend(ig)
38 A	even though	'iːvn ðəʊ	obwohl, obgleich
	reliable	rɪ'laɪəbl	zuverlässig
	to regret	tə rɪ'gret	bedauern
	to announce	tʊ ə'naʊns	ankündigen, melden, mitteilen
	delay	dɪ'leɪ	Verspätung, Verzögerung
	to warn	tə 'wɔːn	warnen, aufmerksam machen
	moustache *(BE)*, moustache *(AE)*	mə'stɑːʃ 'mʌstæʃ	Schnurrbart
	to ring *(BE)*	tə 'rɪŋ	anrufen *(Telefon)*
	to call *(AE)*	tə 'kɔːl	anrufen *(Telefon)*
	while	waɪl	während
	operator	'ɒpəreɪtə	Telefonist(in)
	to reverse the charge	tə rɪ'vɜːs ðə 'tʃɑːdʒ	ein R-Gespräch führen
	call collect (*or:* collect call) *(AE)*	'kɔːl kə'lekt	R-Gespräch
	toll-free	'təʊl 'friː	gebührenfrei
	to dial	tə 'daɪəl	wählen *(Telefon)*
	old movies *(AE)*	'əʊld 'muːvɪz	alte Filme
	to cry	tə 'kraɪ	weinen, schreien
	to make s.b. cry	tə meɪk sʌmbədɪ 'kraɪ	jdn. zum Weinen bringen
	to rejoin s.b.	tə 'riː'dʒɔɪn	sich wieder anschließen, zurückkommen
	engaged *(BE)*	ɪn'geɪdʒd	belegt, besetzt *(Telefon)*
	busy *(AE)*	'bɪzɪ	belegt, besetzt *(Telefon)*
	to cancel	tə 'kænsl	streichen
38 B	to flow	tə 'fləʊ	fließen
	contract	'kɒntrækt	Vertrag
	territory	'terɪtrɪ	Gebiet
	time zone	'taɪm zəʊn	Zeitzone

	false	fɔ:ls	falsch
	to recognise	tə ˈrekəgnaɪz	erkennen
38 D	politely	pəˈlaɪtlɪ	höflich
	firmly	ˈfɜ:mlɪ	bestimmt, entschlossen
38 E	National Anthem	ˈnæʃnəl ˈænθəm	Nationalhymne
38 F	Easter	ˈi:stə	Ostern
	to support	tə səˈpɔ:t	unterstützen
38 H	frequently	ˈfri:kwəntlɪ	häufig
38 J	to board	tə ˈbɔ:d	an Bord gehen, einsteigen
	final call	ˈfaɪnl ˈkɔ:l	letzter Aufruf
	gate	geɪt	Flugsteig
	take-off	ˈteɪkɒf	Start
	airport lounge	ˈeəpɔ:t ˈlaʊndʒ	Wartehalle eines Flughafens
	crew	kru:	Besatzung, Mannschaft
	upright	ˈʌpraɪt	senkrecht, aufrecht
	position	pəˈzɪʃn	Stellung
	safety precautions	ˈseɪftɪ prɪkɔ:ʃnz	Sicherheitsbestimmungen
	folks *(colloq.)*	fəʊks	Leute
	to extinguish	tʊ ɪkˈstɪŋgwɪʃ	auslöschen
	standstill	ˈstændstɪl	Stillstand
38 K	figures	ˈfɪgəz	Zahlen
	in brackets	ɪn ˈbrækɪts	in Klammern
	area code	ˈeərɪə kəʊd	Ortskennzahl *(Telefon)*
	prefix	ˈpri:fɪks	Vorwahlnummer; Vorsilbe
	long-distance call	lɒŋˈdɪstəns kɔ:l	Ferngespräch
	to connect	tə kəˈnekt	verbinden
	transfer-charge call *(BE)*	trænsˈfɜ: (trɑ:nsˈfɜ:) ˈtʃɑ:dʒ kɔ:l	R-Gespräch
	reversed-charge call *(BE)*	rɪˈvɜ:st ˈtʃɑ:dʒ kɔ:l	R-Gespräch
38 L	booked out	ˈbʊkt ˈaʊt	ausgebucht
	sold out	ˈsəʊld ˈaʊt	ausgebucht
	fair	feə	Messe, Ausstellung
38 M	stranger	ˈstreɪndʒə	Fremder
	loudspeaker	ˈlaʊdˈspi:kə	Lautsprecher
	employee	emplɔɪˈi:, ɪmˈplɔɪi:	Angestellte(r)

UNIT 39

New York: Lower Manhattan with World Trade Center

(CB) New York is the financial, commercial and cultural centre of the nation. Its port, stock exchanges, libraries, museums, theatres and restaurants make it one of the world's most exciting cities.
In 1624 Dutch settlers purchased the island of Manhattan from the Indians for the legendary sum of $25. They called it New Amsterdam. Forty years later they surrendered to English troops and New Amsterdam was renamed New York. From the very beginning New York was the most cosmopolitan centre in the New World. New York City is made up of five boroughs – Manhattan, Brooklyn, Queens, the Bronx and Staten Island – with a total population of over eight million. Manhattan is the real heart of the city. There are busy avenues and squares, like Fifth Avenue, Broadway and Times Square. Here the visitor will find the Empire State Building, the United Nations headquarters on the East River and Central Park. Harlem, the largest black community in the United States, is on the Upper East Side. At the southern end, in Downtown Manhattan, is the financial district with Wall Street and the World Trade Center, New York's tallest office towers. At the entrance to New York Harbor stands America's most famous landmark, the Statue of Liberty.

39 A **Out to brunch** oo

(J = Jane, R = Russell, B = Bob, K = Kathy)

(Jane and Russell jogging in Central Park on a Sunday morning; a dog barking persistently.)

J Leave me alone!
This park doesn't belong to you.
Go away!

R Hey, Jane! Don't run so fast.
We're not training for next year's Marathon, you know.

J I was running away from that dog.
You know I hate dogs.

R And I love them. Man's best friend.

J Yes. You always say that. Anyway, we'd better hurry. We've got to go to Bob and Kathy's. Remember?

R Ah, yes. I remember. We've been invited to Bob and Kathy Johnson's flat –

J Apartment, not flat.

R Apartment, then. And I'd rather be at your friends' apartment than jogging around Central Park.

In Central Park, New York

(At Bob and Kathy's apartment)

B Hi, Jane! It's great to see you.

J Hello, Bob. Hello, Kathy.

K Hi, Jane!

J Bob, Kathy – this is a friend of mine, Russell Grant.

R How do you do?

B Pleased to meet you. How are you?

R Er – We're both very well, thank you.

K Well, come on in!

J I'm so sorry we're late.

K Oh, don't mention it. You're not late. Say! You sure look great, Jane.

J Yes. We've been jogging in the park. Russell –

R What a lovely place you've got, Bob!

B Glad you like it. But the apartment isn't our own. It belongs to Kathy's mother.

K It's really my Mom's place. But we look after it for her. Would you like to look around?

J Oh, that would be nice.

R Yes. That would be very kind of you.

B Er – Kathy, darling. We'd better go. It's nearly midday, and you know Bartleby's gets crowded Sundays.

J Bartleby's?

B Yes. That's where we're going for brunch.

R Brunch?

K Oh! Brunch is kind of half breakfast and half lunch. We always go out for brunch on weekends. Then we don't have to make our own breakfast or lunch.

R Actually, I haven't had breakfast yet.

B No problem, Russell! Bartleby's is New York's best restaurant for breakfast or brunch.

R I'd rather have breakfast, if you don't mind.

(A dog barks)

J Is that a dog?

K Yeah. That's the Kramer's dog, in the next apartment.

J Have you got a dog?

K Oh, yes. We have a dog of our own. Buster. Right now he's at my sister's. She's having a doggy party.

J A doggy party!

K Sure! Doggy parties are this year's new fashion. If the dogs get on well together, their owners will do the same.

J Er, yes. I'm sure they will.

R Jane doesn't like dogs. She'd rather have a cat.

J And Russell hates cats. So we've never had a cat of our own.

R Nor a dog. What a pity! A dog is –

J – man's best friend. That's what Russell always says.

B Come on, you guys! It's time to go.

Manhattan, New York

(In Bartleby's restaurant)

K This omelette's good. Are you enjoying yours, Jane?

J Well, I'm having a little difficulty.

B What's wrong there, Jane? Do you need another fork? Take one of ours.

J Thank you. But I'd rather have a knife.

B Oh, I see! You British sure use a lot of knives when you eat. You'd better take mine, Jane.

J That's very kind of you. I don't want to cause any trouble.

B No trouble at all. You're most welcome. How's your fried egg, Russell?

R Fine, thanks.

K Russell, I see you ordered yours sunny side up.

R Sunny side up?

K Yes. Fried on one side. I always have mine over easy – done on both sides.

R Oh, I see.

J Bob, you're not eating your brunch? Do you feel all right? You're not ill, are you?

B No. I'm not sick. I'm fine, thanks.

J Would you like your knife back? Here! You'd better have it back.

B No. That's all right. I never eat much in restaurants.

J But – but you've ordered a lot of food. Eggs –

B Yes. Eggs Benedict. Buster loves his Eggs Benedict. On English muffins, of course.

K Here you are, darling. Buster's bag.

R Buster's?

B Sure! It's his doggy bag. Don't you have doggy bags in Britain?

J No, we don't.

K Oh, you should have them. You put all the food you don't eat into a bag, and take it home for the dog, and –

J We haven't got a dog. Remember?

B But – er – man's best friend.

R That's what I always say, Bob. Here! Take some of mine. For Buster!

K Gee, Russell. That's so kind of you, but –

B I don't know how to say this, but you see Buster likes his –

K He'd rather have –

J I know. He likes his eggs over easy.

Brooklyn Bridge, New York

39 B Questions

Name five famous places or buildings in New York City.
What's the real heart of the city called?
What do you associate with Wall Street?
What do Jane and Russell do before they go to Bob and Kathy's?
What is the word "brunch" a mixture of?
Who's Buster?

39 C And you?

Would you like to live in a big city or would you rather live in a small town?
State the pros and cons.

39 D "would rather" / "had better"

I'd rather have a cup of coffee.	*Ich würde lieber eine Tasse Kaffee trinken.*
Wouldn't you **rather** have a cat?	*Hättest du nicht lieber eine Katze?*
We'd better go now.	*Wir sollten jetzt wirklich gehen.*
Hadn't you better take an umbrella?	*Nehmen Sie nicht besser einen Schirm?*

"I would rather" bedeutet "I'd prefer to have", *ich ziehe etwas vor, ich hätte etwas lieber.*
"Had better" drückt eine dringende Empfehlung, einen Rat, die Einsicht in eine Notwendigkeit aus.
In der Umgangssprache verkürzen wir zu "I'd rather" bzw. "I'd better". Das Verb steht in der Grundform ohne "to".

39 E Rewrite the sentences:

Use expressions with "would rather" or "had better":

We ought to go now.
I'd prefer to have lunch.
They'd prefer to stay in New York.
You should stop jogging.
She shouldn't use this phone.
He'd prefer to come at five.
Russell would be wise to lock up his money.

39 F "own"

New York has **its own** symphony orchestra.	*New York hat sein eigenes Symphonieorchester.*
I'd like to have a car **of my own.**	*Ich hätte gern ein eigenes Auto.*

"Own" kann nur in Verbindung mit einem besitzanzeigenden Fürwort (my, your, his, her, its, our, their) stehen. Die Nachstellung von "of + my, your etc. + own" ist nur bei Substantiven möglich, die mit dem unbestimmten Artikel (oder einem Zahlwort) verbunden werden.

Translate:

Unsere Tochter hat ihr eigenes Zimmer.
Er ist sein eigener Chef.
Wir haben jetzt ein eigenes Haus.
Das ist mein ganz eigenes Rezept. (recipe)
Jeder amerikanische Staat hat seine eigene Regierung.

39 G Use of the "s"-genitive — Verwendung des Genitivs mit 's

Our friends' dog.
Bob and Kathy's dog.
We're not training for **next year's Marathon.**
Bartleby's is **New York's** best restaurant for brunch.

Zur Bildung des Genitivs siehe Band 1, Unit 3 sowie Band 2, Unit 14.
Beziehen sich mehrere Eigennamen auf etwas Gemeinsames, erhält im britischen Englisch meistens nur das letzte Wort die Genitiv-Endung, z. B. Bob and Kathy's dog. Im amerikanischen Englisch dagegen ist auch Bob's and Kathy's dog möglich. Den 's-Genitiv findet man auch häufig in Verbindung mit Zeitangaben und Städtenamen, vor allem dann, wenn ein Superlativ folgt: New York's best restaurant.

39 H Use the "s"-genitive in your translation:

eine Woche Urlaub
das älteste Pub in Dublin
ein Monatsgehalt
ein halbstündiger Fußmarsch
die diesjährigen Konzerte im Central Park
die heutige Tageskarte (Speisekarte)
New Yorks höchster Wolkenkratzer
die aufregendste Stadt der Welt
der Gewinner dieses Jahres

39 I Eating habits in the USA (CB)

Brunch is a mixture of a late breakfast and an early lunch, traditionally eaten on Sundays and served from 11 a.m. to 3 p.m. You can order eggs "your style", e. g. scrambled, boiled, sunny side up (fried on one side), over easy or easy over (fried on both sides), or you can order omelettes or pancakes with maple syrup. All this is served with buttered toast and jelly, the American jam. In many American restaurants you can't just go in and sit down. You'll often find a sign "Please wait to be seated". So a hostess or captain will escort you to a table.
After you've sat down, you'll be brought a glass of iced water without asking for it.
Americans eat everything they can with a fork in their right hand. They only use a knife to cut up their meat. Then they put the knife down and eat with the fork only.
When you want to pay you ask for the "check", the American word for "bill". There'll be tax added to the check but no service charge. An easy way to work out the tip is to double the 8 % tax marked on your check.

39 J Differences between British and American English

Complete the following sentences:

In a London restaurant you ask for the bill, in a New York restaurant you ask for the ......
Londoners take the Underground, New Yorkers take the ....
In America toast is eaten with jelly, in Britain toast is eaten with ......
In a London high-rise building you take the lift to the 7th floor, in a New York skyscraper you take the .... to the .... floor.
Apartment is the .... word for the British word ......
If you dial a number and you can't get through, Americans say the line's .....; in Britain they say it's ....

39 K An invitation to lunch

25 June 19..

Lynn Hyatt
61st Street
15 Central Park West
New York, N.Y. 10023

Dear Lynn,

I'll be staying in New York for a couple of days next month and was wondering if you could have lunch with me. It's such a long time since we met and I'm very anxious to hear how things are with you. What about Tuesday, 17 July? If this would suit you, I suggest we meet in the bar of the Mayflower Hotel at 12.30.

If you could manage it, I'd be delighted.

Yours,
Humphrey

Write a reply to the above invitation.

39 L Situation – Say it in English

Ihr Gesprächspartner fragt Sie, wie es Ihnen geht.
Sagen Sie, daß es Ihnen sehr gut geht.
Sagen Sie, daß dies eine Freundin von Ihnen ist.
Sagen Sie, daß die Wohnung nicht Ihnen gehört.
Sagen Sie Ihrem Gesprächspartner, daß er blendend aussieht.
Sagen Sie, daß das nicht der Rede wert ist.
Sagen Sie, daß Sie heute lieber zum Abendessen ausgehen.
Sagen Sie Ihrem Gesprächspartner, daß es Ihnen lieber wäre, wenn er hier drinnen nicht rauchen würde.
Raten Sie Ihrer Freundin, daß sie zum Frühstück besser ein weich gekochtes Ei bestellen sollte.

39 M Summary ○○

Russell and Jane are jogging in New York's Central Park. They're on their way to Bob and Kathy's. Jane is being chased by a dog. Russell loves dogs, but Jane prefers cats. Bob and Kathy have got a dog called Buster, but at the moment he's at a "doggy party" at Kathy's sister's. Bob and Kathy have invited Jane and Russell to Bartleby's, one of New York's best restaurants for "brunch".
Bob says they'd better set off, as it's getting late. At Bartleby's Jane finds it difficult to eat everything with only one knife – she'd rather have one for each dish, as is normal in Britain. Bob doesn't eat much, although he's ordered a lot of food. He's brought a "doggy bag" to give his food to Buster. Russell offers Bob some of his fried egg for Buster, but Bob doesn't take it – Buster prefers his eggs over easy!

Any leftovers?

Vocabulary			Wortschatz
39	financial	faɪˈnænʃl	finanziell, Finanz-
	commercial	kəˈmɜːʃl	geschäftlich, kommerziell, Handels-
	port	pɔːt	Hafen
	stock exchange	ˈstɒk ɪkstʃeɪndʒ	Börse
	exciting	ɪkˈsaɪtɪŋ	aufregend
	Dutch	dʌtʃ	(Adj.) holländisch; (S) Holländer(in)
	settler	ˈsetlə	Siedler, Kolonist
	to purchase	tə ˈpɜːtʃəs	auf-, ankaufen
	Indian	ˈɪndɪən	(Adj.) indianisch; (S) Indianer(in); (Adj.) indisch; (S) Inder(in)
	legendary	ˈledʒəndrɪ	legendär, sagenhaft
	to surrender to	tə səˈrendə tʊ	sich ergeben, kapitulieren
	troops	truːps	Truppen
	to rename	tə ˈriːˈneɪm	umbenennen
	cosmopolitan	kɒzməˈpɒlɪtn	weltbürgerlich, kosmopolitisch
	to be made up of	tə bɪ ˈmeɪd ˈʌp əv	bestehen aus, sich zusammensetzen aus
	borough	ˈbʌrə	Stadtbezirk
	avenue	ˈævənjuː	Hauptstraße, Allee
	United Nations	jʊˈnaɪtɪd ˈneɪʃnz	Vereinte Nationen
	community	kəˈmjuːnətɪ	Gemeinschaft
	upper	ˈʌpə	ober(e)
	southern	ˈsʌðən	südlich
	downtown	ˈdaʊntaʊn	im tiefer gelegenen Teil der Stadt, im Geschäftsviertel
	district	ˈdɪstrɪkt	Bezirk
	World Trade Center	ˈwɜːld ˈtreɪd sentə	Welthandelszentrum
	Statue of Liberty	ˈstætjuː əv ˈlɪbətɪ	Freiheitsstatue
39 A	brunch	brʌntʃ	Frühstück und Mittagessen
	to jog	tə ˈdʒɒg	laufen, joggen
	dog	dɒg	Hund
	to bark	tə ˈbɑːk	bellen
	persistently	pəˈsɪstəntlɪ	beharrlich, andauernd, unentwegt
	leave me alone	ˈliːv mɪ əˈləʊn	laß mich in Ruhe
	to train	tə ˈtreɪn	üben, trainieren
	to look after	tə lʊk ˈɑːftə	sich kümmern um
	to look around	tə lʊk əˈraʊnd	sich umsehen
	darling	ˈdɑːlɪŋ	Liebling
	to get crowded	tə get ˈkraʊdɪd	voll werden
	to get on well together	tə get ɒn ˈwel təgeðə	gut miteinander auskommen
	owner	ˈəʊnə	Besitzer

	cat	kæt	Katze
	nor	nɔː	und (auch) nicht, noch
	omelette	ˈɒmlɪt	Omelette
	fried egg	ˈfraɪd ˈeg	Spiegelei, Setzei
	eggs sunny side up *(AE)*	egz ˈsʌnɪ saɪd ˈʌp	Spiegeleier
	eggs over easy *(AE)* (*or:* eggs easy over)	egz ˈəʊvər ˈiːzɪ	auf beiden Seiten leicht angebratene Spiegeleier
	muffin	ˈmʌfɪn	flaches Gebäck
39 B	to associate	tʊ əˈsəʊʃɪeɪt	*hier:* (gedanklich) verbinden, in Verbindung bringen
	mixture	ˈmɪkstʃə	Mischung
39 C	the pros and cons	ðə ˈprəʊz ən ˈkɒnz	das Für und Wider
39 F	symphony orchestra	ˈsɪmfənɪ ɔːkɪstrə	Symphonieorchester
	recipe	ˈresɪpɪ	Rezept
39 H	skyscraper	ˈskaɪskreɪpə	Wolkenkratzer
	winner	ˈwɪnə	Gewinner
39 I	(soft) boiled	ˈsɒft bɔɪld	(weich) gekocht
	pancake	ˈpænkeɪk	Eier-, Pfannkuchen
	maple syrup	ˈmeɪpl ˈsɪrəp	Ahornsirup
	jelly	ˈdʒelɪ	*(AE)* Marmelade, *(BE)* Gelee
	hostess	ˈhəʊstɪs	Empfangsdame
	captain	ˈkæptən	Empfangschef
	to escort	tʊ ɪˈskɔːt	begleiten
	iced	aɪst	eisgekühlt
	check	tʃek	*(AE)* Rechnung
	tax	tæks	Steuer
	service charge	ˈsɜːvɪs tʃɑːdʒ	Bedienungsgeld
	tip	tɪp	Trinkgeld
	to double	tə ˈdʌbl	verdoppeln
	to mark	tə ˈmɑːk	auszeichnen, verzeichnen
39 K	I'd be delighted	aɪd bɪ dɪˈlaɪtɪd	ich würde mich sehr freuen
39 M	to be chased by	tə bɪ ˈtʃeɪst baɪ	verfolgt, gejagt werden von
	to set off	tə set ˈɒf	sich auf den Weg machen
	dish	dɪʃ	Gericht; Teller
	leftovers (pl)	ˈleftəʊvəz	Überbleibsel, (Speise-)Rest

Wortschatzregister

Die Zahlen verweisen auf die entsprechenden Abschnitte in den Units, in denen ein Wort oder Ausdruck in einer bestimmten Bedeutung zum erstenmal vorkommt.

Abkürzungen:
S = Substantiv
Adj = Adjektiv
V = Verb
Hv = Hilfsverb
pl = Plural

A

able 32A
above all 28
accept (V) 37J
accommodation 27C
according to 33N, 34A
action 31A
activity 32
admit (V) 36N
advance 27B
advert 27N
advertise (V) 36E
advertisement 34A, 36
advice 35M
advise (V) 29A
agent 37F
agree (V) 28A
aid (S) 30L
alive 38
be allowed to 32A
amateur 29B
amendment 37
announce (V) 38A
announcement 30L, 37A
anti-Irish 35
anxious 36L
anybody 29A
apartment 27A
apologise (V) 28A
appear (V) 27J
architect 37A
architectural 37H
architecture 28
area code 38K
argue about (V) 33A
argument 33L
armchair 29A
armour 28
arms 28
around 32A, 32J
arrange (V) 27A
arrest (V) 33A
artist 37A
arts 37H
ashamed of 28E
assemble (V) 37
associate (V) 39B
assure (V) 36A
at all 27A
at least 27A
attractive 27A
audience 28A
author 35K
automatic 29A
autumn 27A
available 27A
avenue 39
away 27A

B

bad 27A
bank 28
barbecue 32K
bark (V) 39A
basin 38
bathroom 27A
beach 30F
bear (V) 34K
become (V) 27, 30A
bedroom 27A
besides 30
bet (V) 30A
Bill of Rights 37
blow open (V) 33A
blue 34L
board (V) 38J
boiled 39I
booked out 38L
borough 39
bow tie 28A
brackets 38K
branch 33
brand 36A
break into (V) 33A
breakdown service 31F
broadcast (V) 36
brochure 35A
brother-in-law 35M
brunch 39A
brush (V) 36A
bucket 32A
building 27
burglar 29H
burglary 33A
busy 38A

C

cable television 36
call (V) 38A
call collect 38A
calm down (V) 33A
camera 30A
camping equipment 34A
can 36A
cancel (V) 38A
candidate 31
captain 39I

cash on delivery 34A
cat 39A
cathedral 35K
Celtic 35
centimetre 27G
central heating 27A
centre (V) 35
certain 37
change (S) 31A
chapel 28
characterise (V) 32B
charge (S) 37J, 38A
charge (V) 37J
charity 30L
chased by 39L
chat (S) 32B
check (S) 39I
cheer up (V) 30A
cheque 34A
cheque card 34A
choose (V) 29A
Christianity 35
circulation 30
claim (V) 38
clean (V) 36A
cloth 36A
coast 37
collect (V) 27A
collection 28, 37H
colony 37
combination 33A
come on (V) 37A
come out (V) 30A
comment (S) 37L
comment on (V) 30
commercial 39
commercials 36
common 37
Common Market 35F
community 39
company 29A
complaint (S) 34A
complete 28O
completely 31A
confederation 37
congress 37
connect (V) 29A, 38K
cons 39C
consider (V) 30L
constituency 31
constitution 35J, 37
consumer 36N
contact (S) 32
contain (V) 30, 33N
context 36B
contract 38B
contribution 35K
control (V) 28I
control panel 29A
convenient 29A
conveniently 27A
convention 37
convince (V) 36N
convinced 29M
copy 28A
coronation 28
cosmopolitan 39
cost (S) 27A
cost of living 31A
count (V) 32E
county 35
courtyard 38
cover s.th. (V) 30, 30A
cream 35A
credit 37A
Creole 38
crew 38J
crime 31J
critical 36A
cross 35A
crowded 39A
cry (V) 38A
cry out (V) 33N
cultural 30, 37H
culture 37H
cupboard 33A
curtains 27A
custom 38
cut down (V) 32A
cut oneself (V) 28A
cute 37A

D

daily paper 30
damage (V) 37A
dangerous 33A
dark 29A
darling 39A
daughter 34A
day-trip 35A
dead 37A
deal 36A
dean 35K
decent 34A
Declaration of Independence 37
defend (V) 35K
definition 33C
delay (S) 38A
delighted 39K
delivery man 34A
democracy 31
deposit 27B
design (V) 37A
developing countries 30L
development 29, 29A
dial (V) 38A
diamond necklace 33A
die (of) (V) 28B, 35
difference 27M
difficulty 31A
dime 37J
dinner-jacket 28A
disagree (V) 30M, 37K
disaster 28A
discover (V) 29
discovery 29
discuss (V) 31I, 32G
dish 39L
display (V) 29
display (S) 35

distance 34
distant 35A
distinguish 36B
district 39
documents 33A
dog 39A
double (Adj) 29H
double (V) 39I
down payment 27A
downtown 39
drapes 27A
draw up (V) 37
drawing 37I
dress (V) 28A
dress up (V) 32J
drink bar 29A
drip (V) 32A
drive mad 32A
drive off (V) 33A
Dutch 39

E

earnest 35K
at ease 28N
Easter 38F
Easter Rising 35
editor 30A
effort 32M
either 30M, 31A
elder 35A
elect (V) 31
election 31, 31A
election campaign 31A
electrical 34I
electricity 29B
electromagnetics 29B
electronics 29
elevator 27A
elsewhere 36C
embarrassing 28A
emigrate (V) 35, 35A
employee 38M
employer 36B
engaged 38A
engaged in s.th. 33L
enormous 28A
entrance 37A
envelope 34A
equal (V) 27F
equally 36N
equipment 34I, 36A
era 35
escort (V) 39I
establish (V) 37
even if 27
even though 38A
event 30, 33B
evidence 33A
exactly 29A
exchange (V) 34H
exciting 39
exhibition 37A
explanation 37L
explore (V) 38
explorer 28
expression 27O, 34J
extension 27N
extinguish (V) 38J
extra 32H
eyewitness 33K

F

facilities 27L
fact 33
fail (V) 31F
fair (Adj) 31H
fair (S) 38L
fall (S) 27A
false 38B
famine 35, 35A
fancy 28J, 35A
favour (S) 32A
federation 30A
fence 32
fetch (V) 28A
feudal system 35
few 27
fiction 33
field 29B
fight against (V) 28A
figures 38K
final call 38J
financial 39
find out (V) 33A
firm (S) 27A
firmly 38D
flat 27, 27A
flow (V) 38B
flu 30A
fly-killer 36A
folks 38J
follow (V) 28, 35A
fool 28A
for instance 27O
forbid, forbade, forbidden (V) 37A
forecast 33K
Foreign Secretary 30A
forgetful 29A
forgive, forgave, forgiven (V) 27A
former 29A
foot, pl feet 27A
found (V) 37H
fractions 27D
free sample 36A
freedom 37
frequently 38H
fried 39A
friendly 32
in front of 31A
front page 30A
furniture 27J
future 32A

G

gadget 29A
Gaelic 35J
garage 36N

gate 28A, 38J
general election 31
generally 27
gentleman, pl gentlemen 28A
get (V) 37A
get away (V) 33A
get back (V) 33A
get in (V) 31A
get on (V) 28A, 39A
get on with s.b. (V) 33D
get open (V) 33A
get out of (V) 31A
get rid of (V) 33A
glass door 33A
glasses 28A
grammar school 29A
go ahead (V) 35A
go up (V) 27, 31A
go with (V) 34A
gold 35A
gram(me) 27G
grant (V) 35
grateful 28A
great-great-grandfather 35A
ground floor 27A
grow (V) 37
grow up (V) 33
guarantee (S) 36A
guarantee (V) 37
guard (V) 28
gun 33
guy 35A

H

hand-wiping cloth 36A
hands 28J
hang, hung, hung (V) 37A
harbour 37
hardly 33
Head of State 35
headline 30A
head office 30
heavy 32A
help oneself to (V) 28A
helpful 32
hemisphere 37H
heritage 38
hey 34A
hi 35A
high 27A
high-rise building 27
hoarding 36
hockey 32A
hold (V) 32J
honour 38
hostess 39I
house (V) 28
household 29A
housewarming party 32J
housewife, pl housewives 36A
housework 36A
however 27
humanist 28
hunger 31J
hurt oneself (V) 28A

I

iced 39I
identification card 37J
illustrate (V) 35
image 33
imagine (V) 28A
immediately 33N, 34A
immense 28A
importance 35K
impress (V) 33
imprison (V) 28
improve (V) 29A
in advance 27B
in return 35
inch 27G
include (V) 37H
income 31A
income tax 31A
independence 37
Indian 39
individual 37
Industrial Revolution 29
industry 29
inflation 31J
inform (V) 30
information 27N, 30B
ingredients 36A
inhabit (V) 35
inner 28
innovation 35
insist on (V) 37A
instance 27O
instead 27
institute 28A
instructions 36A
intensify (V) 35
interrupt (V) 30A, 36
introduce (V) 28A
invent (V) 29
inventor 29A
Irish 35
issue (V) 35I

J

jelly 39I
jewellery 33A
jewels 33A
jog (V) 39A
join (V) 32J, 37
joke (V) 30A

K

keep (V) 35A
keep down (V) 31A
keep up (V) 31A
killed 37A
kilometre 27G
kingdom 35
knee 34H
know off by heart (V) 28A

L

label 34H
landmark 37H
law 38
lead to (V) 27A
learn (V) 30I
leftovers (pl) 39M
legend 35K
legendary 39
let out (V) 37L
liberty 37
librarian 29A
library 29A
lie down (V) 29A
lie with (V) 31
life, pl lives 32
lift (S) 27A
lift (V) 32A
limited 29A
literature 35K
litre 27G
living 29A
living area 27H
local authority 31A
local elections 31A
located 27A
lock up (V) 33A
locomotive 29
lonely 32
long-distance call 38K
look after (V) 39A
look around (V) 39A
look forward to (V) 34H
look up (V) 28A
loose 37
Lord Chancellor 28
lorry 27A
loudspeaker 38M
lounge 38J
lunchtime 30A

M

machine 29, 29A
mad 32A
made up of 39
magazine 30C, 36
mail order 34
main 31C, 38
majority vote system 31
make s.b. cry (V) 38A
manage (V) 32J
manufacturer 34H
manuscript 35, 35A
maple syrup 39I
mark (V) 39I
masterpiece 37H
match (V) 34A
matter 31I
measure (V) 27A
measurements 27G
medieval 37H
member 28A
Member of Parliament 31
mess (S) 32M
method 36N
metre 27G
midday 30I, 39A
mighty 37
millimetre 27G
Minister of Transport 30A
mistake 27A
misunderstand (V) 27O
mix up (V) 27B
mixture 39B
momentarily 37A
monastery 35, 35A
monk 35, 35A
monstrous 30L
monthly 29A
monument 35
mood 30O
moonlight 30A
motto 31A
moustache 38A
movies 38A
muffin 39A
multi-million-pound business 34

N

nasty 30O
National Anthem 38E
naturally 36A
nearly 28A
necessarily 32F
necklace 33A
neighbour 27A
neither (of) 35M
network 36
news desk 30A
nickel 37J
Nobel Prize 35K
none 29B, 36A
non-profitmaking 36
nor 39A
Norman 28
notice (V) 37L
nought 27G
novelist 35K
nowadays 28
nuclear physics 29
nuclear war 31J
number plate 33K
nut 32M

O

object 37I
obliged 33A
obvious 29M
occupant 35
occupation 35
odd 27K
officer 33
omelette 39A
once 27A
onwards 37
operator 38A
opposite 28I
originate (V) 34
ought to (Hv) 32A
outer 28
over easy 39A

overalls 31A
overlook (V) 34M
overturn 34E
owner 27, 39A
owner-occupied flat 31F

P

page 29A
paint (V) 37A
painting 37A
pancake 39I
panel 29A
parliamentary 31
particularly 35, 37K
partition 35
party 31
party list 31
pass (V) 29F
past (Adj) 27
patron saint 35B
peaceably 37
penicillin 29
pensioner 30L
people 27
persistently 39A
persuade (V) 36C
phew 32A
photography 29
physicist 29B
physics 29A
picture 30B, 33
pink 34J
place (V) 34A
playwright 35K
pleasant 27A
pleased 27O, 29A
pleasure 36A
plenty 35A
plumber 32A
plus 27A
point 33J
police 33
police station 33A
polish (V) 36A
politely 38D
political 30
politician 31A
politics 30, 30A
port 39
position 38J
possibly 33M
postage 34A
powder 36A
power 28
power-loom 29
precautions 38J
pre-Christian 35
prefix 38K
prehistoric 35A
president 29H, 37
print (V) 30
printing 29
prison 28
prisoner 28
prize 35K
proclaim (V) 35
product 36
profound 35
promise (V) 31L, 38A
pronounce (V) 35A
pros 39C
protect (V) 37A
protection 35A
protest (V) 30L
Protestant 35
provisional 35
public 31I
published 30M
pull out (V) 33A
pull oneself together (V) 28A
punctual 29A
punt 35I
purchase (S) 37J
purchase (V) 39
purpose 35D
purse 31A
put back 37A
put off 30A
put on 33A
put up 31A

Q

quality 30, 34A
quantity 34A
quarrel about (V) 37L
quarter 27A, 37J

R

radio transmitter 33A
rag 32A
rain (S) 28A
razor 28A
reach (V) 35
reaction 35
reader 30
real 28A
reality 33
reason 29K
reasonable 27A, 34J
rebel (V) 37
receive (V) 29M
recipe 39F
recite (V) 28A
recognise (V) 33N, 38B
record (S) 35A
reduce (V) 31A
Reformation 35
refund (V) 34H
regalia 28
regret (V) 38A
regular 29A
rejoin (V) 38A
related to 35J
relatives 35A
relax (V) 30O
reliable 38A
relics 35
religion 37

remain (V) 35
remind (V) 28A
remote-controlled 29A
rename (V) 39
rent (S) 27, 27A
replace (V) 28A
reply (V) 31L
report (of, on) (V) 30B
represent (V) 31
representative 37
research 29A
restore (V) 37A
reverse (V) 38A
reversed-charge call 38K
review (S) 30
revolution 29
revolving door 33K
riches 35A
rights 37
ring (S) 33A
ring (V) 38A
rise (S) 31A
rob (V) 31E
robber 33B
rose (S) 32A
round tower 35, 35A
rub (V) 36A
rugby 32A
ruin (S) 31A
ruin (V) 31A
rule (V) 35

S

safe (S) 33A
safe (Adj) 37J
safety 38J
sail (V) 37
saint 35
salary 29A
sale 34E
salesman 36N
sales representative 36A
sample 36A
satisfied 36A
save (V) 31A
scene 35
scientific 30B
scriptures 35A
sculpture 37A
sea 30A
season 27I
secret (S) 37L
secret service 33
security 37A
see (V) 29A, 30F
selling methods 36N
sensational 30
separate 37
sergeant 33N
service 32H
service charge 39I
set off (V) 39L
settle (V) 35, 38
settler 39
settlement 37
shake (V) 28J
share (V) 32C
shave (V) 28A
shock 30O
shoe-cleaner 36A
shoe polish 36A
shout (V) 28I
show (S) 30A
shrink-proof 34H
sick 28A
side 31A
sights 28C, 35A
signal 33A
silver 35A
similar 34H
sincerely 29A
sit up (V) 29A
situation 29B
skill 37I
skyscraper 39H
small print 36A
smart 34A
smashing 32L
so far 27A
so that 27
soft 39I
sold out 38L
sound (V) 28A
southern 39
space 30B
space flight 29
spare (V) 31A
speech 28A
spend (V) 30L
spinning-machine 29
sponsor 36
spoonful 35A
spray (V) 36A
spread, spread, spread (V) 37
spring 27I
spy 33, 33A
square foot 27H
stand (V) 32A
standstill 38J
starvation 35
state (V) 29K
statue 39
steal, stole, stolen (V) 33A
steam-engine 29
step through 28A
stock exchange 39
Stone Age 35
straight 29A
straight away 33A
stranger 38M
strength 32A
strong 32A
subject 28A, 29M
subway 27A
success 36N
sudden 30O
suddenly 37L
suit (V) 34A
Sunday paper 30
sunny side up 39A
superman 35K

support (V) 38F
sure 27A
surrender to (V) 39
surroundings 27L
swimsuit 33K
symphony orchestra 39F
system 31

T

table 34A
tackle (V) 31A
take for (V) 33A
take off (V) 30A
take-off (S) 38J
take over (V) 30A
talent 29M
talk about (V) 33A
talkative 35M
tap 29A
taste 27A
tax 39I
teabag 33K
tea-towel 32A
tear (V) 28A
technology 30
tenant 27
term 27B
terrace 30A
terrific 32L
territory 38B
test (V) 36A
textile industry 29
theatre-goer 33K
thriller 33
tie (S) 34A
tie (V) 28A
till 30A
times 27A
tiny 34A
tip (S) 29A, 39I
toaster 34I
toll-free 38A
toolbox 32A
toothbrush 34I
top 32A
total 27H
touch (V) 37A
tour (S) 35A
Tourist Board 35C
Tourist Office 35A
towel 32A
trademark 36B
train (V) 39A
trained 29A
transfer-charge call 38K
transport 30A
traveller's cheque 37J
treasure 37H
tremendous 32M
tribe 35
troops 39
trouble (V) 36A
trousers 34A
truck 27A
try on (V) 34J
tuning (S) 27A
turn (S) 32A
turn down (V) 33D
turn off (V) 32A
turn over (V) 29A
turn round (V) 28F
type (V) 28A
type out (V) 28A

U

unable 30B
unemployment 31J
unfair 31A
unfortunately 32M
unfriendly 32
uniform 28
United Nations 39
unless 29F
upper 39
upright 38J
upstairs 27A
useless 36A

V

valuable 33A
value added tax 33K
valued object 37I
vast 38
vote for (V) 31A
voter 31B
voyage 37

W

walk (S) 27A
war 31J, 35
warn (V) 38A
wash (V) 28A
wax 36A
welcome 37A
western 37H
westward 37
wherever 30
while 30A, 38A
whisk(e)y 35A
whistle (S) 33A
wide 27A
winner 39H
wipe (V) 36A
wise 36A
wit (S) 35K
without 33
witness 33A
working conditions 33E
World Trade Center 39
worth 35A
wrench 32A
write down (V) 33A
writer 35K

Y

yard 27A

Z

zone 38B

Aussprachehilfen zu Eigennamen

James Baker	ˈdʒeɪmz ˈbeɪkə
Bartleby's	ˈbɑːtlbɪz
Alexander Bell	ælɪgˈzɑːndə ˈbel
Bensons	ˈbensnz
Anne Boleyn	ˈæn ˈbʊlɪn, bʊˈliːn
British Broadcasting Corporation	brɪtɪʃ ˈbrɔːdkɑːstɪŋ kɔːpəreɪʃn
Jack Brown	ˈdʒæk ˈbraʊn
Buster	ˈbʌstə
Edmund Cartwright	ˈedmənd ˈkɑːtraɪt
Christopher Columbus	ˈkrɪstəfə kəˈlʌmbəs
Edward	ˈedwəd
Michael Faraday	ˈmaɪkl ˈfærədeɪ
Finnegans Wake	ˈfɪnɪgənz ˈweɪk
Alexander Fleming	ælɪgˈzɑːndə ˈflemɪŋ
Dorian Gray	ˈdɔːrɪən ˈgreɪ
Guggenheim Museum	ˈgʊgənhaɪm mjuːˈzɪəm
Gulliver's Travels	ˈgʌlɪvəz ˈtrævlz
James Hargreaves	ˈdʒeɪmz ˈhɑːgriːvz
Catherine Howard	ˈkæθrɪn ˈhaʊəd
Jackson's	ˈdʒæksnz
Thomas Jefferson	ˈtɒməs ˈdʒefəsn
Jim	dʒɪm
Joneses	ˈdʒəʊnzɪz
James Joyce	ˈdʒeɪmz ˈdʒɔɪs
James Madison	ˈdʒeɪmz ˈmædɪsn
Kathy	ˈkæθɪ
Marathon	ˈmærəθən
Napoleon	nəˈpəʊljən
Sir Thomas More	sə ˈtɒməs ˈmɔː
St. Patrick	snt ˈpætrɪk
Pilgrim Fathers	ˈpɪlgrɪm ˈfɑːðəz
Pygmalion	pɪgˈmeɪljən
Sir Walter Rale(i)gh	sə wɔːltə ˈrɔːlɪ
Fred Roberts	ˈfred ˈrɒbəts
George Bernard Shaw	ˈdʒɔːdʒ ˈbɜːnəd ˈʃɔː
George Stephenson	ˈdʒɔːdʒ ˈstiːvənsn
Jeremy Swallow	ˈdʒerəmɪ ˈswɒləʊ
Jonathan Swift	ˈdʒɒnəθən ˈswɪft
Taoiseach	ˈtiːʃək, ˈtiːʃəx
Tudor	ˈtjuːdə
Ulysses	juːˈlɪsiːz, ˈjuːlɪsiːz
Vikings	ˈvaɪkɪŋz
George Washington	ˈdʒɔːdʒ ˈwɒʃɪŋtən
James Watt	ˈdʒeɪmz ˈwɒt
Oscar Wilde	ˈɒskə ˈwaɪld
William the Conqueror	ˈwɪljəm ðə ˈkɒŋkərə
Frank Lloyd Wright	ˈfræŋk ˈlɔɪd ˈraɪt
William Butler Yeats	ˈwɪljəm ˈbʌtlə ˈjeɪts
Yeomen Warders	ˈjəʊmən ˈwɔːdəz

Aussprachehilfen zu Orts- und Ländernamen

Atlantic	ət'læntɪk, ə'tlæntɪk
Belgrave Mews	'belgreɪv 'mju:z
Bloody Tower	'blʌdɪ 'taʊə
Bond Street	'bɒnd stri:t
Broadway	'brɔ:dweɪ
Bronx	'brɒŋks
Brooklyn	'brʊklɪn
Burlington Arcade	'bɜ:lɪŋtən ɑ:'keɪd
Canterbury	'kæntəbrɪ
Cashel	'kæʃl
Clonmacnois	klɒnmək'ni:ʃ
Darlington	'dɑ:lɪŋtən
Diamond Row	'daɪəmənd 'rəʊ
Dublin	'dʌblɪn
Dun Laoghaire	dʌn 'lɪərɪ
East River	'i:st 'rɪvə
Fifth Avenue	'fɪfθ 'ævənju:
Fleet Street	'fli:t stri:t
Glendalough	glendə'lɒk, glendə'lɒx
Harlem	'hɑ:ləm
Holyhead	'hɒlɪhed
House of Commons	'haʊs əv 'kɒmənz
House of Lords	'haʊs əv 'lɔ:dz
Houses of Parliament	'haʊzɪz əv 'pɑ:ləmənt
Jamestown	'dʒeɪmztaʊn
Jersey	'dʒɜ:zɪ
Jervyn Street	'dʒɜ:vɪn stri:t
Kells	'kelz
Kensington High Street	'kenzɪŋtən 'haɪ stri:t
Knightsbridge	'naɪtsbrɪdʒ
Leeds	li:dz
Liffey	'lɪfɪ
Limerick	'lɪmərɪk
Lincoln Center	'lɪŋkən sentə
Louisiana	lʊi:zɪ'ænə
Manhattan	mæn'hætn
Manchester	'mæntʃɪstə
Massachusetts	mæsə'tʃu:sɪts
Mayflower	'meɪflaʊə
Mellifont Abbey	'melɪfɒnt 'æbɪ
Metropolitan Museum	metrə'pɒlɪtn mju:'zɪəm
Mint Street	'mɪnt stri:t
Mississippi	mɪsɪ'sɪpɪ
Moissant International Airport	'mɔɪsnt ɪntə'næʃnəl 'eəpɔ:t
Munster	'mʌnstə
Newgrange	nju:'greɪndʒ
New Orleans	nju:'ɔ:lɪənz
Pacific	pə'sɪfɪk
Philadelphia	fɪlə'delfɪə
Plymouth	'plɪməθ
Queens	kwi:nz
Regent Street	'ri:dʒənt stri:t
St. John's Chapel	snt 'dʒɒns 'tʃæpl
Shannon	'ʃænən
Spain	speɪn
Staten Island	'steɪtn aɪlənd
Statue of Liberty	'stætju: əv 'lɪbətɪ
Stockton	'stɒktən
Times Square	'taɪmz 'skweə
Trinity College	'trɪnətɪ 'kɒlɪdʒ
Virginia	və'dʒɪnjə
Wall Street	'wɔ:l stri:t
Water Lane	'wɔ:tə 'leɪn
White Tower	'waɪt 'taʊə
World Trade Center	'wɜ:ld 'treɪd sentə

Erklärung der grammatischen Bezeichnungen

verwendete Bezeichnung	englische Bezeichnung	weitere Bezeichnungen
Bedingungssätze	conditional clauses	Konditionalsätze
Bruchzahlen	fractions	
Fragepronomen	interrogative pronouns	Interrogativpronomen
abhängige Fragesätze	dependent questions	indirekte Fragesätze
Kausalsätze	reason clauses	Nebensätze des Grundes
Konjunktionen	conjunctions	Bindewörter
Konzessivsätze	concessive clauses	einräumende Nebensätze
Passiv	passive (voice)	Leideform
Relativpronomen	relative pronouns	bezügliche Fürwörter
entbehrliche Relativsätze	non-defining relative clauses	
notwendige Relativsätze	defining relative clauses	
Self-Pronomen	self-pronouns	Reflexivpronomen, rückbezügliche Fürwörter
Temporalsätze	time clauses	Nebensätze der Zeit
unbestimmte Pronomen	indefinite pronouns	
unvollständige Hilfsverben	auxiliaries	Modalverben
Verben mit zwei Objekten	verbs with two objects	Verben mit zwei Ergänzungen
Verben mit Zusatzwörtern	phrasal verbs	zusammengesetzte Verben
verstärkender Gebrauch von "do"	emphatic "do"	
Verlaufsform der Zukunft	future continuous	
vollendete Zukunft	future perfect	
Wiederholungszahlen	adverbs of number	

Unit 27

27 B He wants to sell his piano.
Because he mixed up the terms first floor and ground floor. In America they say first floor for the ground floor and second floor for the first floor.
Because the American doesn't like the curtains in the flat. (They're not his taste. He wants to buy new ones.)
He's the tenant. Because he pays rent.
A down payment is a sum of money paid in advance (also called a deposit).

ꝏ **27 E** four ninths – two sevenths – three fifths – a half – two thirteenths – seven eighths – five twelfths – a (one) fortieth – three sixteenths – six tenths.

27H The total living area is 812.76 square feet.

ꝏ **27 J** The flat is on the 5th floor.
They live at 27 Jervyn Street.
The advertisement appeared on August 8.
They'll move the furniture by lorry.
The American is looking for a flat in London.
Russell looked at the American with surprise.
Russell wants to sell the piano by next week.

27 K available

27 N I arrived three quarters of an hour ago.
I'm in London on business once a year.
My rent is £200 a month.
The central heating will be one fifth more this year than last year.
Could I have extension 233 (two double three), please?
I'm calling (ringing, phoning) about your advert(isement) in the local paper.
How far is it to the nearest Underground?
Could I come and see the flat on Saturday morning?
(Can I make an appointment to see the flat on Saturday morning?)
Friday evening is all right as well. (. . . is also fine. . . . would also be convenient.)
Thank you very much for the information.

Unit 28

28 B It has been a fortress, a royal palace, a zoo, and a state prison.
I (one, you) can see the Crown Jewels and the National Collection of Arms and Armour.
William the Conqueror began to build the Tower.
King Henry VI, King Edward V, Anne Boleyn, Catherine Howard.
He's a Professor of History.
He had been reciting (learning) his speech.
He cut himself with his razor while he was shaving.
Because it's too tight. (He doesn't feel comfortable in it.)
The meeting starts at half past six.
Because he's caught a cold and he's torn his jacket.

QO **28 G** They enjoyed themselves at the party.
We found ourselves in the wrong flat.
I can't remember your name.
He's caught a cold.
She introduced herself to the audience.
I must apologise for being late.
He sat down.
Help yourself (yourselves) to a cigarette.
You've got to dress.
He hurt himself with his razor.
Have we got to do it all by ourselves?
She cut herself with a knife the other day.
He can't afford to buy a new jacket at the moment.

QO **28 I** Russell couldn't control himself.
The two men didn't get on very well. In fact, they disliked each other.
They shouted at each other.
The one sitting opposite Russell couldn't pull himself together.
They saw themselves (each other) in the mirror.
The members introduced themselves to each other.

28 J Sie machte sich Sorgen um seine Gesundheit.
Sie trafen sich gestern. (Sie lernten sich gestern kennen.)
Rühr dich nicht!
Du hast dich sehr verändert.
Sie lieben einander sehr.
Ich hoffe, du erinnerst dich an ihn.
Stell dir vor! Ich habe £1.000 im Fußballtoto gewonnen.
Habt ihr euch auf der Party vergnügt?
Versuche immer, du selbst zu sein.
Heute morgen habe ich mich schnell gewaschen und rasiert.
Dann habe ich mich angezogen.
Sie schüttelten einander die Hände. (Sie gaben sich die Hand.)

ΩΩ **28 K** You asked me to remind you about the meeting.
Do you remember what time it starts?
I must remember to take my glasses with me.
It's a good thing you reminded me to take my books.
"We remind visitors that the Tower gates close at five o'clock."

28 L

to measure	– to find out the exact size
to check	– to check something is right
to complain	– to say you don't like something
immense	– enormous
to apologise	– to say you're sorry
splendid	– wonderful
to agree	– to have the same opinion

28 N Would you like some more tea? Help yourself to some more tea.
Help yourself to some cake.
I can't remember my neighbour's name.
Would you please remind me to take my glasses?
I don't feel comfortable in this suit. (I don't feel well . . ., . . . at ease . . .)
I caught a cold when I was walking home in the rain last night.
I don't want to make a fool of myself at the conference tomorrow.
You should be more careful. (You ought to be . . .)
I must apologise for being late. (I'd like to . . ., I'm sorry I'm late.)
I think this evening is going to be a disaster.

Unit 29

29 B It was James Watt. (James Watt developed the steam-engine.)
He built it in the 18th century.
I can see them (some famous inventions) in the Science Museum.
Cartwright invented the power-loom.
Alexander Bell built the first telephone.
No, he doesn't. (He's an amateur inventor.)
He hasn't sold any yet. (None.)
She works at the local library as a librarian.
It's an automatic page-turner.
He could apply for a regular job.
He's Russell's former physics teacher.
Michael Faraday was a famous physicist. He lived in the 19th century.
His field was electricity, especially electromagnetics.

ꝏ **29 E** If you hurry, you'll catch the train.
We'd invite you to stay if we had a larger house.
You'd learn English more quickly if you went to Britain.
He would enjoy this if he were here.
If you were interested in a job, you could send your application to our Research Department.
Would he get angry if I told him about it?
Don't miss the Science Museum if you go to London.
If you don't hurry, you'll be late.
If you don't apologise, he will never speak to you again.
If you could help me, I would be very grateful.

ꝏ **29 F** You can't buy the refrigerator unless you've got the money.
You can't drive a car unless you've passed your driving test.
You won't pass your examination unless you work hard.
I'll be in London by 5 o'clock unless I miss the train.
It won't make proper coffee unless there's enough water in it.

29 H What would you do if you lived in London?
What would you do if you were President of the USA?
What would you do if you had a million dollars?
What would you do if you got a ticket for speeding?
What would you do if you heard a burglar in your neighbour's flat?
What would you do if you were late for a meeting?
What would you do if the price of petrol were double what it is now?

29 J

to wonder	– to ask oneself
to speak to	– to talk to
to expect	– to wait for
useful	– helpful
proper	– real
to improve	– to make better
salary	– the pay for a month's work

29 L I'd like to speak to Mr X.
I've got an appointment to see him.
Pleased to meet you.
It would be useful if we had a machine like that in our office.
Perhaps my firm (company) might be interested in it.
If I were you, I'd improve this machine.
(I'd advise you to improve this machine.)
I'm sure it would sell then.
How do you earn your living?

Unit 30

30 B *The Daily Telegraph* is a daily paper, a quality paper, a serious paper.
It's a paper with big headlines, a lot of pictures and short, simple articles.
These papers give a lot of space to the reporting of sensational events.
Sunday "sister" papers: the *Sunday Telegraph, The Sunday Times,* the *Sunday Express,* the *Sunday Mirror.*
The *Daily Mirror* has got a larger circulation.
No, it isn't. It also provides political, scientific and cultural information.
Because two colleagues of his are unable to come and he's got to do their work.
He'll be in Manchester and he'll be reporting on the annual conference of British engineers.
She'll be covering the Flower Show.
(She'll be reporting on the Jersey Flower Show.)

ꝏ **30 F** I'll be working tomorrow.
I'll be working hard this time next week.
Fred'll be covering the story.
She'll be seeing him next Friday.
We'll be going to the cinema tonight.
He'll be coming by train.
I'll be visiting my friends in the States next year.
He'll be taking a week off.
I'll be sitting on the beach this time next week.
I'll be thinking of you.

ꝏ **30 G** When will you be leaving?
Who will you be going with?
Will you be travelling by plane?
Won't you be taking the children?
Where will you be staying?
What day will you be coming back?
Why won't you be staying longer?

ꝏ **30 I** I'll have paid for the car by the end of the year.
You'll have started your holidays this time next week, won't you?
The minister will have opened the motorway by midday.
Russell will have learnt a lot about engineering after his visit to Manchester.
I won't have made my decision until tomorrow evening.

ꝏ **30 K** I'll lend you the money till (until) next week.
Can you return it by next week?
The guests stayed till (until) 10 o'clock.
Please send us your application by 15 January.
We'll be staying in London till (until) Christmas.
He's on holiday till (until) 25 August.

30 N When will you have finished your work?
I'll have finished it by tomorrow evening.
I'll be spending next week in London.
I'm sorry, the editor isn't in. (I'm afraid . . . .)
He'll be coming in the afternoon.
By this time tomorrow I'll be flying to New York. (. . . I'll be on the plane to New York.)
I'll be staying there (for) a week.

Unit 31

31 B It is sometimes called the "Mother of Parliaments" because it is the world's oldest parliament.
They elect a new parliament every four or five years.
He or she must win the majority of votes in a constituency.
Because she was too young. (Because she was under 18.)
They are going from door to door (*or:* from house to house) to introduce themselves and talk to the voters.

QO **31 E** If he had parked the car somewhere else, he wouldn't have got a ticket.
If Russell had lived in the 18th century, he would have invented the steam-engine.
If they had had enough money, they wouldn't have robbed the bank.
If I had time, I would read the paper.
If the weather were fine, I would go for a walk.
If she hadn't won the football pools, she wouldn't have bought this car.
If I had the money, I'd go round the world.
If he had been more careful, he wouldn't have hurt himself.
Russell won't come if you don't invite him.
He could have helped us if he had wanted to.

31 F *(Suggested answers)*
If I had won £50,000 on the football pools, I'd have bought an owner-occupied flat.
If I had missed the plane, I'd have taken the next one.
If I had failed my driving test, I'd have tried again.
If the car park had been full, I'd have looked for another one. (. . . for a space in the street.)
If my car had broken down on the motorway, I'd have called the breakdown service.
If I had had time this afternoon, I'd have come to see you.

QO **31 H** Every four or five years the British people vote in a general election. This election decides who is going to represent the people in the House of Commons.
There are no elections for the House of Lords.
Many people think that the majority vote system is not fair. In Germany, if a candidate doesn't win a constituency, he or she has still won some votes for his or her party and may get into Parliament through the party list. In Britain these votes are lost.

31 K How are you these days?
Not too bad, thank you. Quite well, thanks.
It could be worse.
Do you mind (Would you mind) if I ask you a few questions?
I won't keep you long. (I won't keep you a moment.)
Not at all. (That's all right.)
I don't agree. (Well, actually I don't think so.
I wouldn't say so. I don't agree at all. I disagree with you.)

Unit 32

32 B He's working in his garden (He's having a chat with Jane, with a neighbour of his.)
He's going to mend (repair) the tap in Jane's kitchen.
He must get his tools.
He's ready to help others. (He's helpful.)
She used to play hockey.
It's the plumber's job.

32 E Anyone can learn English if he tries hard enough.
In England you must drive on the left.
It may (might) rain tonight, but I hope it won't.
We must change our clothes for dinner.
You ought to have called the plumber.
May I smoke here? (*or:* Can I smoke here?)
Can you play the violin?
Customers ought to count their change.
Women should earn the same money as men if they do the same job.
If you want to buy a house, you shouldn't spend too much money on travelling.

32 F She ought to have called the plumber. (She should have called . . .)
He ought to have changed the wheel. (He should have changed . . .)
We'd be glad if you could come.
He wasn't allowed to use the towel.
Must he report on the engineers' meeting? (Does he have to . . .?)
You needn't necessarily be punctual.
I won't be able to come.

32 G I had to say goodbye.
He didn't have to mend it.
We had to discuss it again.
She didn't have to do it herself.
It had to have a garden.
They didn't have to worry about it.
It had to be good.

32 H the rush hour – hospitality – a plumber – a neighbour – a tip – surname – a prisoner – a customs officer

32 I

/e/	/iː/	/æ/	/ɑː/
pleasant	mean	stand	can't
ready	please	tap	ask
weather	believe	piano	

/ɔː/	/ɒ/	/ʌ/
call	long	enough
story	sorry	plumber
	cost	cover
	job	trouble
	what	

32 L I used to play tennis.
Could I ask you a favour? (Can I . . .? May I . . . ?)
Could I (might I, may I) ask you to shut the door?
(Could you shut the door, please? Would you . . . .?)
Must you smoke in here?
Are you sure you ought to call the police? (. . . you should call . . . ?)
You may be right.
May I invite you to lunch.
That's great. (. . . smashing, terrific.)

Unit 33

33 B She spent her evening at a party. (She was at . . .)
She came home at 11.30 p.m.
A witness is a person who was present at an event and saw what happened.
The safe was in the cupboard in the living-room.
It belongs to Jane and her husband.
Because she thought there's been a burglary.
They found a radio transmitter.
She was arrested as a spy.
A person who steals something is a thief, or a robber, or (if he breaks into a house) a burglar.

33 E I can't get on with my work.
Why do you put up with such working conditions?
Can you find out who did it?
Did the police manage to get the door open?
The burglars had put the light on.
He couldn't get rid of the piano.
I'll ring him up in a moment.
We were talking about an important problem.

QO **33 G** Who were you smiling at?
Which European language is the easiest to learn?
What colour is your car?
What time did you leave?
Who do you want to lock up?
Which letter is more important, the one to New York or the one to Washington?
Who got away?
Whose is this safe?
What can I show you?
Who helped you with your work?
What do you know about the robbery?

QO **33 H** Who did she go out with?
What (which) books belong to Russell?
Whose key did he give her?
Who did he speak to?
Who were the thieves?
Who does she want to see?
What were you talking about?
Who put the light on?

33 K Augenzeuge – Teebeutel – Badeanzug – Einkaufsliste – Mehrwertsteuer – Drehtür – Nummernschild – Tippfehler – Badehandtuch – Spionagering – Trinkwasser – Theaterbesucher – Wahlvorhersage – Polizeiauto

QO **33 L** What invention are you talking about?
There was an important discovery.
They were engaged in a long argument.
He works in the development department.
You must get medical treatment.
Wouldn't you like to make a little speech?
I wasn't impressed by his strength.
We got an invitation to a dinner-party.

33 M Excuse me, do you happen to know where I can find a (tele)phone box? (...where there is... ?)
Could you possibly tell me where the nearest police station is? (Excuse me, can you tell me where . . . ?)
There's been an accident on the M 4.
Somebody has run into another car.
I'll be a witness if you want (need) one.
Thank you very much (for your help). That's very kind of you.
What was the other car like?
Tell me exactly what you saw.

Unit 34

34 B Because the clothes are much cheaper than in a shop.
(Because they want to save money.)
They want to wear them at (to) a wedding.
They placed the order on August 16.
Russell ordered a dark grey suit with two pairs of trousers, a shirt and a tie.
Jane ordered a red dress and a coat.
They paid by cheque.
They paid £251.50.
No, they didn't. The clothes were too small. They ordered continental sizes instead of British ones.

QO **34 E** I haven't got a coat that (which) matches my new dress.
The car he is driving is not his.
He doesn't know the man who (that) lives next door.
The house we saw in Canterbury is for sale.
The parcel that (which) came this morning was for Jane and Russell.
Jane likes the girl who (that) works in her office.
A lot of tourists who come to London every year want to see the Changing of the Guard.
The car he was driving overturned.
Are you sure this is the book you want?
You can't get alcoholic drinks in restaurants that (which) are not fully licensed.

34 G The catalogue I was looking at.
The stamps Humphrey was looking for.
The man I sold the car to.
The people I work with.
The music you're listening to.
The tickets you asked for. (. . . you were asking for.)
The subject we were arguing about.
The article you didn't agree with.

QO **34 K** He never carries an umbrella.
Russell is wearing a bow tie.
I can't bear this nonsense.
It's cold. Why aren't you wearing a coat?
British policemen don't usually carry guns.

34 L I'm looking for a warm coat.
What size do you take?
I take size 40.
Have you got this coat in other colours?
The blue coat suits you very well.
I'll take this coat. (I'll have this coat, please.)
I'd like a scarf that matches my coat. (. . . that goes with my coat.)
Can I pay by Eurocheque? Do you accept a Eurocheque?

Unit 35

35 B It's Dublin.
It's a part of the United Kingdom.
It's St. Patrick.
Because of the great potato famine.
It's the Prime Minister, in Ireland called "Taoiseach".
One can see the Book of Kells in Trinity College, Dublin's University.
The Easter Rising was in 1916.

ꝏ **35 F** People who come to Ireland usually want to see Clonmacnois.
Ireland, which is a member of the Common Market, is an independent country.
Trinity College, which houses the Book of Kells, is Dublin's University.
Are you the gentleman whose car is parked on the double yellow lines?
The man they met in the pub was an American.
Where's the book I gave you?
St. Patrick, who lived in the 5th century, is Ireland's patron saint.
Dublin, which lies on the River Liffey, is the capital of Ireland.
He's a man whose words you can believe.
The General Post Office, which was the scene of the Easter Rising of 1916, is a historic monument.

35 H We've no idea where to go. (We don't know . . .)
I've no idea who to invite. (Could you tell me . . .)
I've no idea when his birthday is. (Could you tell me . . .)
I've no idea what to do. (I don't know . . .)
I've no idea why he works on Sunday. (I don't know . . .)
We've no idea what to see in Dublin. (Could you tell us . . .)
I've no idea when the plane takes off. (Could you tell me . . .)
I've no idea what to suggest. (I don't know . . .)
I've no idea how to get there. (Could you tell me . . .)
We've no idea when to go to Ireland. (Could you tell us . . .)

35 L Hello. It's nice to see you. (It's a pleasure to see you.)
I'm so glad you could come.
Excuse me, haven't we met before?
What a surprise! Fancy meeting you here!
Help yourselves to some drinks.
I must be off now. (I have to go now. I must go now.)
It's a pity (that) you can't stay longer.
You must come again soon.
You're always welcome.
Thank you very much for a lovely evening.
Can I give you a lift?
That's extremely (awfully) kind of you.
Not at all.

Unit 36

36 B He's a sales representative.
It's "Wonderhelp", a kitchen and household equipment firm.
She bought him some car wax.
It's a trademark, a name of a manufactured article, a special name for an article to distinguish it from other goods.
Because his car didn't start. (. . . wouldn't start. Because he wanted to use Jane's phone.)
I can see them in newspapers, on television, in the Underground.
No, it doesn't. It gets its money from the government.

QO **36 E** How much does that car wax cost?
We're staying in Brighton for a few days.
May I have a little more milk, please?
I haven't much time for playing tennis.
There are a lot of fine shops in London.
Have you read many books so far this year?
There were only a few people in the restaurant.
How many chairs are there in this room?
There's very little sugar in my tea.
I've had a little trouble with my car this morning.
Many firms pay a lot of money to advertise their products on television.
There's only very little bread in the house.

QO **36 H** Would everybody listen, please?
Jane goes to work every morning.
These shirts cost £15 each.
Has either of your parents visited you?
They seem to be afraid of each other.
Jane and Russell see each other every day.
You can come on Monday or Tuesday, either day is fine.

QO **36 J** Graham explained everything to his students.
Russell asked Jane a lot of questions about the car.
We paid him a visit.
Humphrey reported the accident to the police.
Jane sent her friends some picture postcards. (*or:* . . . sent some picture postcards to her friends.)
Jane made us a steak. (Jane made a steak for us.)
Why didn't you introduce me to all your friends?
Are you writing this letter to your brother?
Show it to me.

36 L Haben Sie für mich eine Zeitung zum Lesen?
Sie haben es ermöglicht, daß Sie unsere neue Broschüre über Irland bekommen.
Das Beste, das wir tun können, ist selbst dorthin zu gehen.
Ich mache mir Sorgen (bin besorgt), ob das Bild rechtzeitig fertig wird.
Das Paket ist zu schwer für Sie, um es hochzuheben.

36 M Have you got a few moments to spare? (Could you spare (me) a few moments?)
Yes, what is it?
I've got some samples for you to try out.
I (can) assure you that these articles are excellent.
I'm not so sure about that. (I doubt it.)
How do you know?
I can make you a special offer.

Unit 37

37 B The "Mayflower" was the ship in which the Pilgrim Fathers sailed to America.
Thomas Jefferson.
The Constitution, the Bill of Rights.
America has got 50 states (at present).
He was an American architect who designed the Solomon R. Guggenheim Museum in New York City.

37 E Catalogues are sold by the entrance.
The museum had been opened in 1959.
A special exhibition is going to be shown next month.
Yesterday a picture was damaged.
The police were called.
The painting will be finished soon.

37 G The special exhibition was opened yesterday.
Has Jane been informed?
Everything will have been done (completed) by the 25th.
Who's going to be invited? (Who should be invited?)
I won't see him.
When was the house built?
The museum was closed on Monday.
The museum was closed at five o'clock.

37 I to establish – to found
something made with very great skill – masterpiece
to plan – to design
a person who produces paintings, drawings or other works of art – artist
a highly valued object – treasure
to show – to present

37 K It's a great place (a wonderful room).
Van Gogh's paintings are shown on the third floor.
It's a fine work of art.
What do you think of Picasso's paintings (pictures)?
I like the early works of Picasso. (. . . Picasso's early works.)
I don't particularly like these drawings. (. . . don't like . . . much.)
I don't like modern art.
I disagree with you. (I don't agree with you.)
I see what you mean. (I see your point.)
Are you sure the museum is closed on Mondays?
(Do you know for certain that . . .?)

Unit 38

38 B The Mississippi.
It was a contract between Napoleon and the United States about the sale of the Louisiana territory.
New Orleans.
It's in the Central Time zone.
Denver, Phoenix.
Because he doesn't want to be recognised. (. . . he doesn't want people to know who he is.)
He's the President of Express Airlines. (. . . of an American airline.)

38 E Maybe there's a delay because the weather's bad.
(Al)though he's wearing a moustache, it's not really his.
We can watch television while we're waiting.
Since (as) it's such a bad airline, why do you fly Express?
As soon as (when, if) he comes, let me know.
Let's have a swim before we have dinner.
When (if) it isn't late, Flight 213 arrives at a quarter to twelve (AE: at quarter of twelve).
After Louisiana had been given back to France, Napoleon sold it to the United States.
When he arrives, the band will play the National Anthem.

38 F We're looking forward to Easter because we're going away for a few days.
Since (as) the courts are under water, we can't play tennis.
(We can't play tennis because the courts are under water.)
(Al)though she was tired, she went to work. (She went to work even though she was tired.)
I was out when he called. (He called while I was out.)
Since (as) the weather was fine, we decided to go for a walk.
(We decided to go for a walk because the weather was fine.)
(Al)though he was hurt, he continued to play. (He continued to play even though he was hurt.)
He couldn't come because he was ill. (As, since he was ill, . . .)
I'll support your idea even though I'm not convinced.
or: (Al)though I'm not convinced, I'll support your idea.

38 H BE
Yesterday I went to the theatre.
The cars blocked the city centre.
The flight was cancelled.
AE
Catalogs are sold over there.
He dialed the wrong number.
There are a hundred centimeters in a meter.
They do have some superb jewelry in Diamond Row.
Free concerts are held frequently at Lincoln Center's Library of the Performing Arts.

QO **38 J** The announcement was made
c) in the airport lounge.
The announcement was about
b) a welcome on board and normal safety precautions.
The captain made the announcement
b) before landing.

38 L I'd like to make a long-distance call to San Francisco.
When does the flight arrive in Denver?
Why is Flight 213 to Denver delayed?
I'd like to make a reservation for a single room for tomorrow night.
I'm sorry, we're sold out (booked out) because there's an industrial fair going on at the moment.
Could (Can) you recommend me another hotel?
The telephone number was always engaged (busy) although I tried several times.
I intend to go to New York next year.

Unit 39

39 B The Empire State Building, the World Trade Center, Broadway, Times Square, Fifth Avenue, the United Nations Building, Central Park, Wall Street.
It's called Manhattan.
Wall Street is the financial district of the City of New York.
(*or:* I associate the Stock Exchange with Wall Street.)
They jog (go jogging) in Central Park.
Brunch is a mixture of "breakfast" and "lunch".
Buster is Bob and Kathy's dog.

QO **39 E** We'd better go now.
I'd rather have lunch.
They'd rather stay in New York.
You'd better stop jogging.
She'd better not use this phone.
He'd rather come at five.
Russell had better lock up his money.

39 F Our daughter has got a room of her own. (. . . her own room.)
He's his own boss.
We've got a house of our own now. (. . . our own house now.)
That's my very own recipe. (The recipe is my very own.)
Every American state has its own government.

ꝏ **39 H** a week's holiday
Dublin's oldest pub
a month's salary (a month's pay)
half an hour's walk
this year's concerts in Central Park
today's menu
New York's highest skyscraper
the world's most exciting city
this year's winner

ꝏ **39 J** In a London restaurant you ask for the bill, in a New York restaurant you ask for the check.
Londoners take the Underground, New Yorkers take the subway.
In America toast is eaten with jelly, in Britain toast is eaten with jam.
In a London high-rise building you take the lift to the 7th floor, in a New York skyscraper you take the elevator to the 8th floor.
Apartment is the American word for the British word flat.
If you dial a number and you can't get through, Americans say the line's busy; in Britain they say it's engaged.

39 L How are you (today)?
I'm very well, thank you.
This is a friend of mine.
The apartment (flat) isn't mine. (. . . doesn't belong to me.)
You look great.
You're welcome. (Don't mention it.)
I'd rather go out for dinner today.
I'd rather you didn't smoke in here.
You'd better order a soft boiled egg for breakfast.

All's well that ends well

Can you help Humphrey with this crossword puzzle?

Across

1 every Englishman drinks it
2 ten cents
5 in unit 33 Jane was arrested as a . . .
6 first name of an American architect – he designed the Guggenheim Museum
7 capital of Ireland
9 short for "Robert"
11 he wrote "Pygmalion"
14 past tense of "run"
15 a famous London department store
16 the time before the present
19 come . . . . 5 o'clock
20 personal pronoun
21 he developed the steam-engine
23 personal pronoun
24 on the condition that
25 preposition
26 person who prepares a newspaper

Down

1 famous people were imprisoned there
3 people who live in Ireland
4 borough of New York
7 the American word for "curtains"
8 auxiliary verb
10 a city in the USA
12 in unit 37 you were taught a lesson about . . .
13 he designed the Guggenheim Museum in New York
17 he wrote *Gulliver's Travels*
18 in unit 32 Russell had to mend a . . .
22 he built the first telephone
25 conjunction

If you put the letters in circles into the right order, you'll get the name of a famous ship.